BLEAK HOUSES

BLEAK HOUSES

Disappointment and Failure in Architecture

Timothy Brittain-Catlin

The MIT Press   Cambridge, Massachusetts   London, England

Excerpt from "Faith Healing" from *The Complete Poems of Philip Larkin* by Philip Larkin, edited by Archie Burnett, copyright © 2012 The Estate of Philip Larkin. Introduction copyright © 2012 Archie Burnett. Reprinted by permission of Farrar, Straus and Giroux, LLC and Faber and Faber Ltd.

"Could It Be Magic" inspired by "Prelude in C Minor" by F. Chopin; words and music by Barry Manilow and Adrienne Anderson. Copyright © 1973 Universal Music— Careers and EMI Longitude Music. Copyright renewed EMI Music Publishing Limited and Universal Music Publishing MGB Limited. International copyright secured. All rights reserved. Reprinted by permission of Hal Leonard Corporation and Music Sales Limited.

MIT Press books may be purchased at special quantity discounts for business or sales promotional use. For information, please email special_sales@mitpress.mit.edu.

This book was set in Adobe Caslon by the MIT Press. Printed and bound in the United States of America.

Library of Congress Cataloging-in-Publication Data

Brittain-Catlin, Timothy.
Bleak houses : disappointment and failure in architecture / Timothy Brittain-Catlin.
pages cm
Includes bibliographical references and index.
ISBN 978-0-262-02669-7 (hardcover : alk. paper)   1. Architectural criticism. 2. Architectural practice. 3. Architecture—Human factors. 4. Architecture and society. 5. Failure (Psychology). I. Title.
NA2599.5.B75 2014
720.1—dc23
2013018083

10   9   8   7   6   5   4   3   2   1

For Keith Diplock

CONTENTS

ACKNOWLEDGMENTS

This book was written during study leave kindly granted for the purpose by the Kent School of Architecture and the Faculty of Humanities at the University of Kent, and I would like to thank my Head of School, Professor Don Gray, for his generous and trusting support throughout. It is also a pleasure to have another opportunity to thank Alastair Service, who introduced me to Edwardian architecture some 35 years ago.

Many people have been extremely helpful to me during the writing of this book, and some have saved me from embarrassing errors and omissions. My thanks to my brother William Brittain-Catlin and to Rupert Thomas, the editor of *The World of Interiors* and my loyal patron, for reading and commenting on some of the chapters. I am particularly grateful to Edward Bottoms, archivist at the Architectural Association School of Architecture, the school's librarian Eleanor Gawne and photographer Sue Barr, and also to the following: Gerry Adler; Eddie Anderson; Cressida Annesley, Canterbury Cathedral Library; Clive Aslet; Jamie Barnes; Neil Bingham; Shirley and Romanos Brihi; Konrad Buhagiar; Rupert Butler; Mark Connelly; Tim den Dekker; Nick Dermott; Janet Durden Hay; Björn Ehrlemark; Percy Flaxman; Jonathan Glancey; Simon Henley; Henrik Hilbig; Mark Horton; Xavier Iglesias, DPZ; Jonathan Jones; Josh Mardell; Heather Nathan, Yale University Press; Craig Page; Hannah Parham; Ulrik Plesner; Seamus Perry and Anna Sandler, Balliol College, Oxford; Alan Powers; Karen Sampson, Lloyds Banking Group Archives; Paul Sharrock; Rev. Christopher Skingley; Gavin Stamp; Charlotte Stead,

Keswick Museum and Art Gallery; Peter Morris Dixon, Robert A.M. Stern Architects; Louise Velazquez; Tracey Walker, Manchester Art Gallery; Julie Wing; and Ellis Woodman; and to Kurt Helfrich and the staff of the British Architectural Library at the Victoria & Albert Museum and at 66 Portland Place in London. I would like especially to thank my friends Mosette Broderick and Andrew Saint, and my early mentor Peter Blundell Jones, to all three of whom I owe a great deal beyond this book.

I am extremely grateful to Roger Conover at MIT Press for his valued advice and support throughout the execution of this curious project, and to Justin Kehoe, Matthew Abbate, and their team for their efficient management of it. I would also like to thank Gillian Beaumont for her superb copyediting.

But above all I want to express my appreciation to Keith—thanks to whose friendship I have, after what seemed to me like five decades of loserdom, finally become something of a winner myself.

INTRODUCTION

BEING A LOSER

When I returned to England in the middle of the year 2000, after nearly ten years abroad, I discovered that I had become a loser. The local contemporary architectural world that I had known since childhood, and had once been so passionate about, had changed so much that I soon found that I no longer had any interest in or understanding of it. When I had left my homeland at the beginning of 1991, I still had a broad understanding of and sympathy to the things that motivated most architects. Architecture then had been a consolidation of the post-Second-World-War-style consensus, mainly derived from the Scandinavian version of modernism, and it had been refined and developed by architects both consciously and unconsciously over decades. Even after the noisier episodes of postmodernism, buildings had remained by and large orthogonal, with only an occasional and regular curve to them; and those created by architects were, mostly, designed with the declared intention of enhancing the town and the landscape for those who saw them and used them. Even buildings designed by architects without pretensions, or not by architects at all, such as those originating in the back offices of speculative developers, at least had the grace to pretend that they, too, were there for human benefit (and sometimes it was true). There had been ups and downs in quality, with the ups concentrated around the ends of decades and the beginning of the next ones: the late 1950s; the late 1960s; even the late 1970s. But in terms of the big things in life, nothing really had changed since modernism had become the mainstream in England with the development of the first New Towns around London in the late 1940s.

By 2000 this comfortable and reassuring world was fast being pushed aside by a new and aggressive form of architectural design. In September 2001 I started teaching the history and theory of architecture at the Architectural Association School of Architecture (AA) in London, where one saw perhaps too much of the avant-garde or the crest of passing fashion. There were no orthogonal buildings on the computer screens at all. To some extent this was because of the kind of conceptualization that was then dominating teaching: no one expected the youngest students to design buildable objects. That in itself was not particularly frightening. But those who were admired, whether within the school or linked to it, were now working on buildings designed using a process called parametrics. Students happily explained to me that their abstract sketches were turned into improbable, organic forms using computer algorithms that generated and managed shapemaking, so that a design took on a life of its own. The result was a structure where the walls and floors were a peculiar shape that had no historical or contextual connotations to it, and where the function of the building or the logic of the plan was unimportant to the overall design. To me it was unintelligible: not just the process, but the very fact that anybody wanted to make a building in this way.

This made me think about architects such as myself who were forced to face the fact that the rug—of critical acceptance, even of mainstream appreciation—was being pulled out from under their feet. At the time I was researching the Gothic Revival for my doctorate on Augustus Pugin's residential architecture, and I became interested in the pre-Gothic architects of the early nineteenth century. Had they felt the same as me, I wondered, when confronted with the assertive cult of the Gothic Revival? Had they despaired too? Almost certainly. There were some prominent casualties. The most striking of these was George Basevi, best known as the original designer of the Fitzwilliam Museum in Cambridge in 1836, and also of the façades of the houses around Belgrave Square in London. It is well known—it is a canonical moment in the story of the Gothic Revival—that in 1843 Pugin designed a fine set of buildings for Balliol College, Oxford, that were rejected almost certainly because he was a Roman Catholic at a time when conversions to Catholicism posed a real threat to the credibility of Oxford High Church Anglicanism. But what is less known is that Basevi had already been commissioned to design a Gothic-style quad for Balliol, and that Pugin, having seen his proposal, shamelessly and aggressively rubbished it, in a letter to a friend who was one of the fellows.[1] Basevi's project was abandoned as a result. Basevi was a competent designer in the pre-Pugin version of Gothic—"Tudor Gothic"—and although we do not know what he thought of the new, correct, "truthful" version of the style, it is a fair bet that he could not produce it himself, because if he had been able to, he would have done. Perhaps he disliked it; perhaps he was frightened of the leaders of the new Gothic cult, with their moral hysterics and their passions. Tragically, in the true sense of the word, he fell to his death from the roof of Ely cathedral, of which he was surveyor, in 1845. Sometime later George Gilbert Scott restored Ely in the new approved, historically correct, Gothic fashion, and Basevi's modest contributions to it were forgotten. Basevi's fall came as the neo-Gothic reached the final stage of its conquest of English architecture, and marked the beginning of the period in which neoclassical architecture was all but abandoned by high-art people.

As was to be the case again in the first decade of the twenty-first century, the practice and design of architecture changed so fast and so completely that a great number of its talented practitioners were relegated to obscurity. A new category of architect emerged: the loser, the designer who was not part of the dominant clique. Basevi was just one of many. The provinces of all Western countries are full of these

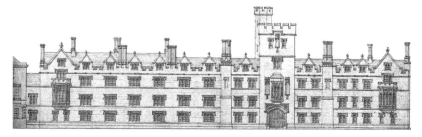

FIGURE 0.1
George Basevi's design for the Front Quadrangle at Balliol College, Oxford, circa 1841.
By kind permission of Balliol College, Oxford.

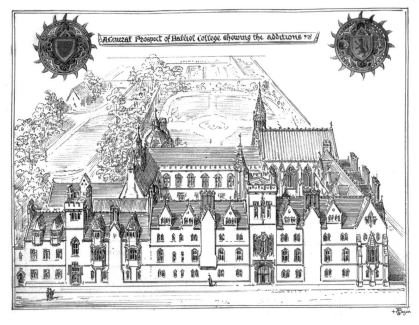

FIGURE 0.2
Augustus Pugin's bird's-eye view of his scheme of 1843 for the same site. By kind
permission of Balliol College, Oxford.

people, who watched as cleverer, more talented, less principled, better-
connected interlopers from capital cities took their jobs away. And
subsequently, even the first rank of provincial English architects who
were classicists—Harvey Elmes, say, or Cuthbert Brodrick—are
pigeonholed into single-line descriptions in mainstream introductions
to the period in which they worked, thanks to the one building they
designed which for some reason or another is unavoidable. And as it
happens, both Elmes and Brodrick ended their lives in circumstances
which contribute somewhat to the "loser" character of their professional achievements.

By contrast, one of the outstanding features of the Gothic Revival
is the youth and the assertiveness of its leaders, the ecclesiologists and
their architects, who in a remarkably short time managed to dominate
the design of churches and much else in England—and subsequently

across the Anglican Church, the British Empire, and beyond. There is no doubt as to the talent involved; in fact their arrival on the scene gave the country a truly fine body of work that is without parallel in any European country in the nineteenth century, and led directly to some of the marvels of the arts-and-crafts era which influenced architecture worldwide. One would have to take a very odd view of history to say that these wide-eyed young men were "wrong," or for that matter that England was "wrong" to have adopted the new style. They were undoubtedly "right": what Pugin achieved, directly or through his personal influence, was astonishing, and enriched what architects did, and the people they built for, without measure. The criticism the Goths leveled at the neoclassical men was, however vicious, nearly always justified: the work was often cheap, or incompetent technically, or simply looked unsatisfactory. Thanks to a series of persuasive writers as much as to a small number of astonishingly dedicated and productive designers, the Goths won the argument. In time these events established a key characteristic of modern architectural criticism: its bombastic, triumphalist, exclusive, moral tone, originally derived from the strident theological debates between evangelicals, Puseyites, and Roman Catholics in the 1830s and 1840s. Alongside this, the early Gothic Revivalists' call for "true" buildings, which emerged from a puritanical English architectural preoccupation with what is sometimes called "realism" in buildings, turned into a shibboleth against which the "honesty" of every single new design was eventually to be measured.[2]

Being good and being right is a perfectly reasonable basis for a history of architecture; and unless young architects are excited or inspired by what they see, in books and magazines as much as in reality, there is little hope for the rest of us. But being good and being right are not the only criteria by which one can write about and explain architecture in the wider context of what the built world means for those who are sensitive to it. This book is an attempt to show how other ways of presenting architecture have been suppressed since Pugin, or have been unnoticed, and how the triumphalism of first the Gothic Revival and then modernism came to dominate architectural criticism and history across the Western world right through to the present time, with no sign of abating yet, at the expense of a quieter and more modest way of looking at and interpreting buildings. It looks into the prevailing macho culture of architecture, and the dubious alliances that architects have made with noisy critics or other people who do not possess the accumulated visual sensibilities that architects have, and whose priorities lie beyond the attractiveness of a building in its own right. It looks at "show trials" and suggests that architectural history has more to offer than what writers have considered "good," "successful," or "influential" architecture. By laying these concepts aside, one can come to a more profound understanding of what it is that buildings can do for those who see them and use them. It asks whether the sadness that architects feel when confronted with their idealized memories of the past and their disappointment and impotence in the face of them has in fact created memorable, profound buildings for them and for the many who see them and use them. If it has a single message, it is that an exploration of the story of an architect's relationship with his or her own building has more to offer than a simplistic teleological or triumphalist approach to architectural criticism, and also suggests a more effective way of talking about buildings to those who have become indifferent to them.

THE BATTLE WITH WORDS

It seems to me that one of the reasons why architects have been consigned to failure is that what they were trying to do did not suit the types of literary priorities that were prevalent at any particular time: their buildings were there to be felt, to be experienced, not to be categorized in fashionable terms. At a certain point even successful and influential architects—Pugin, for example—have been victims of a literary and intellectualizing view of culture as much as their own victims—Basevi, for example—had been before them. Furthermore, the use of words to describe their own buildings by some architects, across the twentieth century from C. F. A. Voysey to Daniel Libeskind, is, although sonorous and inspiring, quite clearly daft and meaningless if interpreted literally.[3]

This is not to say, however, that buildings cannot be presented effectively through words: it is the incompetent way in which some architects and critics do it that is the problem. One of the ideas I shall explore here is that novelists, whose primary tool is language, can indeed describe the architecture of a building in more satisfactory terms than those for whom words are secondary. The use of words and terms by critics can be shallow and limited, especially as they deploy words to denote generalities or categories of things. Furthermore, architects— like, no doubt, other nonliterary people—grab at the words that are in fashion at any given time, and apply them to what they are designing in the hopes of making their designs more comprehensible or justified to the people who have to pay for them or use them. Thus they are at a disadvantage when literary fashions change. I have mentioned that early-nineteenth-century Gothic Revival architects talked about truth, honesty, morality, and so on: they did it because this was the language of their clientele, the predominantly Christian intellectual milieus around them. Early modernist artists and designers did much the same with a different set of terms, but for the same reason. But is the neo-Gothic really about truth or morality? Is early modernism about being functional? Enough people have already pointed out that they were not. They were, like all types of design, about trying to create a particular response through a provocative three-dimensional experience. It is a nonsense to say that architecture is about what architects say about it themselves at any given historical moment, and as much a nonsense to claim (as is done too often, for example by biographers or art historians) that architecture can be judged in literary terms, such as "romantic" or "postmodernist," without the meaning being essentially different from the way such terms are applied in literary criticism or historical investigation.

So it is important to make a distinction between different types of writing. My own teacher, Andrew Saint, urges architectural historians to describe and write about buildings as if telling a story, and this is what he, Mark Girouard, Clive Aslet, Kenneth Powell, and others have done, inspired perhaps by the late John Summerson—all professionals emerging from the English tradition of the enthusiastic amateur or journalist-writer: in fact this approach defines a distinct, popular, and highly regarded school of English architectural history that is continually retrieving forgotten architects from loserdom. Adam Summerfield, a former student of mine, dedicated his undergraduate dissertation to the subject of how planners and developers misjudged the process of public consultation for a prime waterside site in his home town, one of the most economically and socially deprived in the region; their mistake, he said, was to present to local residents drawings of exciting new buildings, which simply aroused antipathy. In fact, he concluded, telling an atmospheric, literary, *story* of what the new development could do would have conveyed the intentions much better—to my mind, a striking and valuable observation from someone who was much more of a designer than a writer.[4] Novelists can do this very well. In particular, there is something about the domestic architecture of the beginning of the twentieth century that has attracted almost continuous attempts at placing the feelings it evokes into words. Look at novels from the early works of H. G. Wells to Alan Hollinghurst's recent *The Stranger's Child*—discussed later—to see the large suburban villa and the small country house of the Edwardian period used directly to convey what Voysey called, with characteristic unhelpfulness, "ideas in things."[5]

Thus it has sometimes seemed that writers such as these novelists, who have few pretensions as architecture critics, have done this job much better than some professional architectural writers, because they have aimed at telling much more of a story than a simple description of a building as a packaged artifact. This story is nothing to do with the biography of the architect; it is to do with the world that architect has evoked. Critics and theorists, by contrast, too often divorce buildings from the emotions that surround them and fall back on simple teleological narratives about style, change, and influence. Popular architectural criticism will remain profoundly shallow if it never catches up with those storytellers who can effectively visualize and project what J. R. R. Tolkien called a "secondary world"—that is, a parallel existence which catches the imagination.[6] Some of the most effective architectural writing is that which establishes a "secondary" world in the minds of those who are reading, coming closest to the visceral, emotional and, above all, associational approach of architects to their own work. Indeed, some architects have also created "secondary" worlds, in buildings and schemes rather than in words, and most likely their appeal to other architects lay in this rather than in any specific concept. So by taking a literary approach to architecture we might discover some lost joys.

Yet architects face a further challenge too, and one that is just as dangerous: a critic may judge that they have become so in thrall to a particular literary tradition that their work has lost the freshness that comes with the direct engagement a creative person has with design. Is this fair, I wonder? A common indication of this is to draw a view of a building in a way that implies that it is rooted in an attractive view of history or a literary narrative: just as Norman Foster and the illustrator Helmut Jacoby put sexy helicopters in their aerial views, so British and American architects of the neo-Regency and Edwardian "Queen Anne" put pert young milkmaids and wooing farmer lads into theirs, alongside rainwater butts and pergolas aplenty. One of the most common arguments against traditionalist and neoclassical designers of all periods is that they are shackled to a sentimental literary-cultural view of life that time and time again blights their buildings: in fact, being "sentimental" is one of the most serious charges made against architects, especially in architecture schools where teachers feel that they have to shock impressionable students away from their natural inclinations. Herbert Baker, Edwin Lutyens's second string on the design of the new government center at New Delhi and the architect of many large institutional buildings, has long been seen as a failure for precisely that reason. His rebuilding of Robert Taylor and John Soane's Bank of England in the heart of the City of London in the 1930s was somehow made so much worse for critics by what was widely seen as his disingenuous attempt at rewriting the building's history from his own perspective: "a masterpiece of egregious diddling" is what Nikolaus Pevsner called it.[7] The critics' automatic condemnation of "sentimentality" is something I shall question, for architects themselves cannot win battles with words, and so long as words are the dominant cultural medium, they are liable to become losers.

FINDING JOY IN SADNESS

My intention is to look at several episodes in architectural history that are centered on architects who fell outside the canon—who were not particularly famous, at any rate outside their immediate circles—and to see what we can learn from them. Certainly their work suffered from not having the strong word-based narrative that the predominant styles enjoyed. But what also holds these episodes together is that they all share the common themes of disappointment and failure, because of the way in which the architects in them tried, unsuccessfully, to create "secondary" or alternative worlds which never came off. These worlds are disappointed and lonely ones, because only the architect and a few others ever inhabited them; and by the conventional standards of architectural criticism they are failed worlds, because they produced no lasting architectural tradition.

The terms "disappointment" and "failure" are not intended to be metaphorical; they are intended to be actual descriptions of what can be seen in buildings. While researching the work of the mainly early-twentieth-century architect Horace Field (1861–1948) I came across the branch of Lloyds Bank that he designed in 1903 for Wealdstone, near Harrow in northwest Greater London. It was intended as a beautiful mirror to a civilized but imaginary life, the village green of the age of Good Queen Anne, but today, mutilated and marooned on a more than usually ugly stretch of English suburban high street, it has become a building that to any but the most insensitive observer is desperately sad. In a sense it always was, because Field's optimistic vision of the world was never going to be realized in the context of an undistinguished London suburb; and, most likely, it always will be, because English Heritage, the government agency responsible for listing buildings of architectural significance, has recently decided that it is not worth protecting.[8] As we will see, it also emerged that this wonderful building was erected pretty much at the point at which Field's promising early career was beginning its downward trajectory.[9] Once we know that Field's career was disappointing, even buildings from his successful years seem to have the seeds of hopelessness in them, and the more one discovers about him, the worse it gets. Even the authoritative biographical dictionary of Edwardian architects illustrates his entry with a building not by him, describing it as "characteristic" of his work.[10]

Some of Field's buildings are sad today because of the modern state of decay or mutilation that they have landed up in, but others are sad because they speak of a freshness, an optimism, an innocence that never came to be fulfilled. Likewise there is a sadness too in books made for interior designers and their clients, of houses so neat and tidy

FIGURE 0.3
Lloyds Bank, Wealdstone, Middlesex, designed by Horace Field, and photographed a few years after its completion in 1905. By kind permission of Lloyds Banking Group Archives.

FIGURE 0.4
Lloyds Bank, Wealdstone, as it appears today, choked by the indifferent architecture of a north London high street. Courtesy of the author.

that they suggest a home without children, or a place where the simple joys of emotional fulfillment remained unanswered and the décor has become a substitute for it: *Romantic Style: Lovely Homes, Pretty Rooms, Gentle Settings*; *The Home Within Us: Romantic Houses, Evocative Rooms*, and *Romantic Irish Homes* are some titles currently being offered, continuing a long tradition; but even looking longingly at authoritative monographs by a capable writer such as Martin Wood, the author of *Sister Parish: American Style*; *John Fowler: Prince of Decorators*; *Nancy Lancaster: English Country House Style*, and so on, seems to suggest a wish to detach oneself from the exigencies of regular life.

Sadness can be found in many places. One of the common aspects of the buildings designed by some of the architects I am going to discuss is that they are trying to fake something which comes naturally to other people. It is a bit like trying to pretend that you are in love, or (sadder still) that someone you love is in love with you. But everyone recognizes the delusion. Either these things are true or they are not: it is all or nothing. In my childhood summer holidays in Scotland we used to look for a sprig of rare, "lucky," white heather among the masses of lilac-colored flowers; sometimes we found a flower that was a very pale lilac, and wondered if it was white, but our aunt told us what turns out to be a great truth in life: you know at once if it is the real thing. Anything else is wishful thinking. Buildings such as Field's bank branches with their Queen Anne airs were wishful thinking too, in the sense that no one was ever going to recognize them as representative of any of the long-term things that architects try to achieve and critics write about. It has taken about a century after the completion of the Wealdstone bank for anyone to refer to Field with anything more than a passing mention.[11] By the conventional standards of architectural criticism Field is a loser, a failure, a faker; and yet his buildings are no less remarkable and memorable because of that. In many cases the feeling is more intense still, because the designer did not have the status, the ability, some particular aspect of the imagination, to join the ranks of the truly capable. These are stories worth telling, and they suggest ways of communicating with those who find design unintelligible.

Some architects have in fact been aware of this sense of loss and failure about themselves: they are only too aware of a moment of the past, or a kind of architecture they enjoyed, or the character of their

own town or of any favorite place, ebbing away from their grasp—
sometimes because of a great turnaround in fashion such as the one I
faced thirteen years ago, or the turmoil of the 1840s or 1920s, or again
in the era of postwar city rebuilding in the 1950s and 1960s. They want
to try to go back and to hold onto something that is slipping from
them: this lies at the heart of the sense of disappointment that engulfs
them and creates that aching feeling we all recognize. It is in this way
that I remember the Commonwealth Institute in Kensington, London,
an exhibition hall in the form of a striking blue hyperbolic paraboloid
designed in 1958 by Robert Matthew, Johnson-Marshall & Partners.
The infantilizing effect it has on me is expressed by the fact that I don't
just want to it to be the same as it always was; I want it to be *exactly* as
it was on those days when my father used to take me on the rare days I
saw him. Or as it was when we went on a trip there from primary
school, when it rained too much for us to play football beside Harrods
furniture depository at Barnes, and we went into the little cinema that
we reached through a dark corridor at the back of the building and saw
the film about the growing of vines, with Prokofiev's First Violin Con-
certo as accompaniment on the soundtrack. And afterward we looked
longingly at the little Commonwealth nation flags for sale in the sou-
venir shop at the entrance, each one slightly more expensive than our
weekly pocket money would allow. This is what I want back. Of course
it is all impossible. It does not help me that today I have enough money
to buy all the flags in the shop. The old place will never come back
because that period in my life will never come back, any more than will
the curious official attitude to the Commonwealth, in which the whole
of Canada got a stall much the same size as the ones dedicated to Hong
Kong or Barbados. Alas for the nostalgic, the interior of the building is
now being changed altogether by John Pawson.

For the failed architects, everything is a kind of hopeless gnawing
at the edge: the key architectural experience in visiting a place, whether
in real life or in the imagination, is one of loss. That, it seems to me, is
at least as important as the historical architectural facts of a building's
modish form, or its imaginative plan, or its place in urban landscape
history, or the subsequent career of its designers, or any one of the various ways in which it has generally been celebrated. When the Commonwealth Institute building was first threatened a few years back, the

Twentieth Century Society, a British amenity society, came rushing to its defense. The people who run this organization are all my age. It was surely the loss of the experience of going there as a child, along the cloistered entrance and down that magical bridge over the shallow pond and in by the darkened hall with its stained-glass windows, and not the building's place in conventional architectural history in design or urban terms, that motivated them. (By contrast, the view of the original project architect, someone who is far from being any kind of loser, was that the campaign for retaining the building was preposterous.)[12] Paul Crampton's recent book *Canterbury's Lost Heritage*, which mourns not only the postwar destruction of beautiful and picturesque historic buildings in that ancient city but also the recent demolition of the plain and cheap Scandinavian-inspired 1950s shops and car parks that replaced them, provides a clear demonstration of the fact that these feelings are to do with personal experience, memory or loss, and not the preference for one architectural style over another, or any of the other logical or organized ways of judging buildings that critics and journalists commonly rely on. Much writing about architecture by laymen is in fact a deep cry from the heart about the loss of dear things and the impossibility of making them anew.

BACKING OUT

Another theme this book looks at is that of serenity, of retrenchment, of retreat and seclusion, all related too to lost innocence and lost childhood. By and large, architecture critics and historians have said little in favor of these; the buildings that strike the eye and attract attention are the lively ones, and it is considered a measure of success that a new building is deemed exciting. Perhaps that was most obviously true in the twentieth century when, for the first half at least, technological changes in daily life were so extreme that it appeared obvious that the buildings which mimicked or reflected them would be the ones that were admired and valued. These buildings were selected and promoted because they were different from, not because they were the same as or variations on, the buildings that preceded them—even if the technological achievements that they represented were in truth transient ones that would scarcely register in any study of technological progress itself.

Again the early nineteenth century provides an interesting commentary. John Claudius Loudon's *Encyclopaedia of Cottage, Farm, and Villa Architecture and Furniture*, published internationally in 1833, marks a milestone in the history of modern domestic design because of the scientific and rational way in which its editor dealt with construction methods and building function, and the incorporation in even small buildings of the latest advances in industrialized components and fittings. Yet any reader will soon realize that Loudon, in common with many other writers of the time, placed a great deal of value on a building conveying a sense of retiral and seclusion, to the extent that achieving these can sometimes be almost a primary aim of the building. During the 1820s and 1830s, when the Tudor and Elizabethan revivals in architecture were much discussed in England, the idea that the old vernacular styles seemed to project an image of serenity, of security, was often referred to positively. For writers of this period, it was the neoclassical styles that seemed brash and outgoing. It took Pugin and the Puginites to turn this upside down. Pugin saw his architecture as an aggressively active one, a way of designing and building that plunged its residents into making public statements about themselves and their way of life. In fact the layout of the large private house, by the end of the nineteenth century, was supposed to demonstrate explicitly the way people lived in it, and indeed in some cases created a type of planning that forced people to turn private events such as religious devotion into public demonstrations, a realization of the evangelical argument that one's private life is a public affair. The idea of retiral as a virtue in architecture soon vanished among the high-art people: tellingly, Voysey maintained that he aimed for it, but no one believed him, because they saw in his buildings not the long, low, horizontal lines of a building at rest, which is what he claimed for them, but a pert and vivid geometry that came as a harbinger of international modernism.[13] As we will see, the traditionalist revivals in domestic architecture that followed the arts and crafts movement or any other burst of modernity have usually included attempts to reestablish retiral and seclusion as positive attributes in buildings, an aim supported enthusiastically by popular publishing on the subject of the small and medium-sized house

on both sides of the Atlantic. A similar phenomenon has been identified by Andrew Dolkart in his study of the changes imposed on Man-
hattan townhouses in the early twentieth century.[14] Most likely the
great majority of clients of domestic architecture were sympathetic; but
critics, and subsequently historians, were not.

In addition to the questioning of the value of assertiveness, novelty,
self-exhibition, and consistency in architecture, there is a further theme
that recurs throughout this book: the dominance of a generally macho
culture in architectural history and criticism. It seems implicit in the
early Gothic Revival, and in some cases it has been blatant, as when the
English Brutalists launched their attack on the slightly earlier generation of Scandinavianists as "effeminate."[15] Modernism may be written
about today in a more critical light than it was in the 1960s, but nevertheless one is struck, for example, by the rapturous descriptions of the
cars, airplanes, and helicopters of Foster that mark recent articles or
books about him.[16] Frank Gehry, according to Francesco Dal Co, "puts
on the classic emblems of aggressive male identity" when he goes out to
play ice hockey.[17] If I have concentrated so far on historical architects
who have been "bullies," it is not hard to find some who are equally
"sissies."

There used to be a simple dichotomy between the "masculine" neo-
Gothic and the "feminine" neoclassical styles, but the situation is more
complicated than that, some styles changing sides according to fashion
and interpretation. The quaint neo-Tudor residential architecture of
the period between the two world wars, now commonly re-created in
Britain and America, provides an example of this. There has been
growing interest—first marginal and now, increasingly, mainstream—
in this style, which was traditionally viewed by high-art critics as the
work of architectural losers divorced from the masculine concerns of
modernism. Now it appears that the neo-Tudor—with its applied
pseudo-timbers and fancy ironwork, its latticed windows with their
stained-glass panels, its Jacobean staircases on a tiny scale, the golf
clubs in the hall, the smell of polish and the folded paper lampshade
over the brass shaft that catches a sunbeam through the casements—
will soon start featuring in historical surveys as something much more
significant to architectural narratives than it ever was at the time. In
order for that to happen, it will simultaneously be translated into a

winners' style; macho, loud, assertive, the style that was intended to project the strong united family, and not, as historians such as Paul Oliver and Gavin Stamp have hitherto maintained, the architectural underdog of the twentieth century.[18] In fact the recent book *Tudoresque*, by Andrew Ballantyne and Andrew Law, has already taken a step in that direction.[19] Looking back now, it appears that the poet John Betjeman's early celebration of it was, among much else, an appeal over the heads of both aesthetes (neo-Regency) and intellectuals (modernist) to what he presumed was the taste of the large majority of "normal" people, family men with proper jobs who spent their Saturdays playing golf or rugby. So at different periods both modernism and the neo-Tudor have been the protagonist in this macho debate and, as with the earlier themes I have suggested above, it is not actually the style itself that matters but the architect's relationship to it.

In some of the other arts, creators and critics alike have been aware of these things: "It seems that once the *violent* has been accepted, the *amiable*, in turn, is no longer tolerable," wrote Igor Stravinsky after hearing of the reception given to concerts by his adversary Pierre Boulez, quoted by Alex Ross, in whose acclaimed recent survey of twentieth-century music this comment became a significant theme.[20] But architecture, as ever, lags behind, its protagonists unable to find a language that expresses what most buildings really do, and what most people want from them. The victims of this approach are, mainly, the modest, the delicate, the decent, the wistful, and the quiet, who continue to be overlooked; this book goes back to see what we have missed out on. The subject may strike some as a pathetically dainty one. In fact the inspiration for putting these thoughts to paper came originally from a derisive comment by the actor Ian McKellen, who was reacting to those who had objected to nudity in one of his performances: "I would love to know who these people are and what kind of dainty world they live in."[21] This book should provide an answer.

1

LOSERS

When I was a student at the University of Cambridge in the early 1980s I was taught by Peter Carl, who used to describe certain themes in architecture as "epiphanic." Because we were British and he was American it sounded to our ears like "epiphonic," to me a word that suited the kind of addictive pop music that makes you feel, when you're elated, that something great is about to happen to you. Anyone my age who listened to the radio, or went out dancing, got that feeling easily and cheaply from the lyrics and the incessantly upbeat disco music of the time and, for that matter, from much of the pop music we had grown up with in the 1960s. If the epiphanies of great architecture were cut from stone and stood out proud on the horizon, uplifting the hearts of generations and calling upon the finest thinkers and writers to extol their magnificence, far cheaper and more easily accessible were those little upward blasts of epiphonic pop, the torch songs, the disco, the fanfares, which promised too easily a happier life that lay just "round every corner."

Except, of course, it almost never did. You went out dancing on a Saturday night with your veins throbbing, but on Monday nothing changed. You turned up and you did your work. Some of it went well, but your life was not transfigured and you were still a mediocre architecture student and not another step down the road to becoming one of the great designers of history. Life is like this for almost everybody: the music, or a similar stimulus from popular novels or films, is consistently deluding us by making us feel that our investments of time and emotion are worth it. But becoming great comes with talent, with some astonishing luck, and with plenty of hard work; it doesn't come from being excited by these sensations. Looking at great buildings brings a buzz too, even from pictures. There are many architects who are excited by big ideas and inspiring buildings, and they want to re-create in their own work this feeling of greatness. They are dazzled, as it were, by the sensations. But they are unable to make it happen themselves because they don't have the talent, and the luck never came to them. Perhaps it came, but then it was cruelly taken away.

They are the losers. They comprise, in fact, nearly all the members of the architectural profession to some degree; but, strangely, architectural history and criticism are almost never about them. The loser-architect is sometimes, but not necessarily, someone whose designs are no good—forgettable, clumsy, or even ugly. There are plenty of people who have made a happy and prosperous career out of that, and we will come to them later. Nor is it the fine designer whose works were admired—eventually, perhaps—to the extent of becoming part of the canon, but whose miserable or empty private life, or terrible end, or debilitating illness, made their own lives unhappy. Charles Rennie Mackintosh, Antoni Gaudí, and Louis Kahn are not by any stretch of the imagination losers. The loser is the person who never got where they wanted to be professionally, or has never been recognized at all for their efforts. The loser is the disappointed non-achiever whose private longing for beauty is appreciated by almost nobody. The loser may have been unable to design or execute the beautiful buildings they dreamed of, or alternatively they may have done exactly that only to find that their work was greeted with sneers for its sentimentality, its gentility, or its lack of imagination, and was written out of history.

The losers tell us a great deal about architecture because of the rich variety of ways in which it is possible to be one. Architectural criticism tends to be triumphalist and macho in tone, singling out a small number of winners who, as they grow in fame, employ press officers to ensure that this very triumphant and macho nature of their buildings reaches even the readers of the tabloids. Simple, powerful messages about architecture are the ones that get remembered. The person with only a general interest in buildings will remember, for example, statistical information—the tallest, the most expensive, the widest span, the most sophisticated technologically. Some readers clock on only when the architectural story is essentially about real estate—in fact, newspaper features on big new developments often omit the name of the architect altogether. Those whose job it is to tell architects about new buildings will identify a simple point—the influence of one of the masters of modernism, a new idea about shape or materials, a new response to an urban condition—and this is the story they will tell as they write. Almost all those who chronicle architecture as it changes over a long period of time choose their canon of buildings teleologically: no one ever seems to have broken out of this. These messages are tough and simplistic: they go one way and they do one thing.

The losers, on the other hand, throw out a wide range of experiences for those who want to get to know buildings better. They offer ways of looking at buildings that can relate much more closely to our own experiences, and give a more accurate picture of the relationship between architecture and the rest of our culture than the old ways. The more one can spot a message of personal failure, the mark of the loser, in a building, the more there is to say about it and the richer the experience the building can bring us. These messages are often about frustration, or loss, or sterility, and each time we recognize or identify one, the window of experience broadens. And that is important, if only because in general, the qualities of architecture are not greatly understood or appreciated by most people, and that leaves architects feeling vulnerable. From this position they ratchet up yet further their distance from society, and those who are capable of it deploy bizarre vocabularies in an attempt to turn their work into a hermetic sacred mystery, and disconnect themselves from what everyone else in their society is doing. And it is important too because it is more realistic: buildings are large, complicated, expensive things, for most people by far and away the single most expensive thing that they have any personal experience of, with so many aspects to them that might go wrong. Creating a building involves an enormous range of decisions and experiences. The single-line descriptions of conventional architectural history cannot begin to get near expressing the cultural richness of any building.

There are many ways in which architects can become losers, and lack of talent or drive is merely one of them. Gifted, hardworking architects can lose battles about style, or politics; they can choose a path which is unpopular or unfashionable, and as a result be pretty much forgotten. They can be a person who recoils from the overwhelmingly macho nature of most architectural criticism, or from the small cliques that influence or even decide what is fashionable. In small countries, for example Israel and the Nordic countries, these cliques can be tiny, a kind of dictatorship of opinion that survives because there is no bulk of opposition to it, or because simple, strong alliances can be forged between cultural critics and politicians. In Israel a capable architect called Shlomo (or Salomon) Gepstein, who built elegant blocks of flats in Tel Aviv in the 1940s and 1950s, found his work satirized and cold-shouldered by the "Hug," the small group of Labor Party-supporting architects favored by the dominant political mainstream, because he was a supporter of the rival political movement; and yet there was no real architectural difference between the type of building he was designing and the ones that they did.[1] Architects themselves, and architectural journalists, continue to choose victims from time to time: Jan Kaplický of Future Systems is an example of the latter whom I will discuss later.

Losers too can be people who are fated to be compared during their lives and long after their deaths with talented people they could not help but be associated with: a parent, a teacher, a student, a son or a daughter. Losers can also be people who know already that they have lost. Maybe they kidded themselves that they were on the way—maybe they persuaded themselves, spread over the drawing board with their big idea for the competition entry, elated, with a glass of wine and uplifting music on the radio, that their career was going to take off— but they knew, in their hearts, that it would not. To know what it is you dream of achieving and to know at the same time that you are perpetually covering up for your inability actually to achieve it is one of the great emotions of life. Wishful thinking will get you nowhere. The architectural loser is like the rejected lover who remembers a few affectionate hugs from the object of his desire, and tries to persuade himself that these were a sign of real love, only to walk around the street corner to discover that same object engaged in a genuine, hot-blooded passionate embrace with the person they have chosen to prefer. No end of talking or persuading will bring him within a mile of the real thing. He is aware of how sad he is, and he cannot hide it.

INTRODUCING THE ULTIMATE LOSER

There are many, many kinds of architectural loser, and it is often possible to find one or two examples who seem to embody whole categories of loserdom.

After the Gothic Revival had taught me about the first wave of architectural loser, I came across someone who is in many ways representative of the second—those condemned in the early twentieth century by the arrival of modernism. I started to study the work of the British late-Victorian and early-twentieth-century architect Horace Field, not least because his name cropped up recurrently in localized studies of Edwardian architecture; yet there was very little information on him, and he was absent from any narrative survey of his period.

In fact Field is a very good example of a failure, precisely because at first sight he does not seem to have been a loser at all. He has two major achievements to his name. The first is that he designed several fine buildings in a photogenic, lush English baroque which were built as he intended; they still stand and are still admired, even by people who are not generally interested in architecture. One of these is the large headquarters of the London and North Eastern Railway at York, designed in 1898–1906 by Field in collaboration with the railway company's architect, William Bell; Field on his own then designed a small London office for the firm in Westminster; several modest houses for up-and-coming politicians in the immediate area; and the headquarters of the Church of England newspaper *Church Times* and the publisher George Bell near Kingsway in London.[2] Most of these received enthusiastic notices from the professional press. Field's second achievement was quieter but far more influential. He designed a small number of prototypical high-street branches for Lloyds Bank, then growing fast from its roots in the English Midlands to become one of the national "Big Five" retail banks.[3] Here he did something novel, which turned out to have a powerful impact on the appearance of every high street in Britain. Up to this point, bank branches had looked like commercial premises, adopting late-Victorian versions of Gothic, Tudor, or neoclassical styles, often somewhat mixed and bastardized. Those done by Lloyds' principal architect J. A. Chatwin in the late nineteenth century were exactly like this: my own local branch, in the Kentish seaside town of Broadstairs, is one of Chatwin's, and it is the ugliest building on the high street. Field's branches, by contrast, were modeled on pretty merchants' houses dating from the Restoration of King Charles II in 1660 up to the mid-eighteenth century, a period of which he, together with his assistant Michael Bunney, made a fine illustrated study, in a book of 1905; a sign of its recurring impact is that *English Domestic Architecture of the XVII and XVIII Centuries* was reprinted in 1928, when the Regency revival was in full flower, and its style and content were imitated in both British and American publications for some time afterward.[4] Field's bank branches had, in most cases, fine red brickwork, restrained and elegant stone dressings, and attractive door surrounds with prominent hood molds and corbels; they sometimes borrowed the more delicate elements of Regency architecture, such as multipaned bow or bay windows, rather as if an architect of 1820 was remodeling a building from a hundred years earlier. We will look later at why Field might have chosen this gentle, charming, hybrid style, but for the present the point is that the other banks rapidly copied it, as did pretty much every other commercial and public building in the many, many new town centers under construction during the interwar boom.

And yet: the remarkable thing about Field is that he ended up a loser. If his achievements fill a single paragraph, the number of things that seem to have gone wrong could fill a book. My primary evidence is that Field registers nowhere in architectural surveys of the period, almost as if he had never existed; even in the most authoritative dictionary of Edwardian architects he is misrepresented. In part that is because the Regency style was never taken seriously by critics once modernism had arrived—we will look at that later—but also because of the way in which Field's career turned out.

In the first place, Field worked in constantly changing partnerships: with Bell, with Evelyn Simmons, with Cyril Farey, with Amos Faulkner, and with Bunney, among others—and presumably as a result there is no clear corpus of work which can be attributed to him, and no surviving single archive. Secondly, it is difficult to trace much of his work: in fact, in one area of Surrey where he built a great deal at the turn of the century the town clerk decided around 1900 to exclude architects' names from building applications in the council's records, and much later his successors decided to dispose of their entire collection of historical plans. Thirdly, many of his buildings have disappeared—a fine pair of French-looking houses he designed in Smith Square in Westminster lasted scarcely twenty years, but quite a few of his smaller houses have disappeared too. Some others have been mutilated.

But Field suffered professional indignities at the time he was working, too, and perhaps because of his own judgment. There are so many that it is difficult to know where to start. His splendid neo-baroque buildings went up before the style became popular; everyone knows that Edwin Lutyens moved from arts and crafts to "Wrenaissance" about a decade after Field had given it up—in 1906, at Heathcote, the large house he designed in Ilkley in Yorkshire—so to know that Field had been and gone beforehand spoils the triumphant, teleological narrative of one of the great masters of architecture. In 1911 Field, with Farey, won a prestigious competition for the redevelopment of Trevor Square in Knightsbridge in London, but the project never got off the ground and he never won a competition again, although he came second more than once. He later did build an imposing terrace in the same style, in Devonshire Street in Marylebone, but the development was never completed; the western end is truncated and the symmetry destroyed. By the 1920s many young architects had adopted his various romantic styles—cottages with formal interiors, Frenchified "Queen Anne" villas—and were doing it better than he was: in fact his name drops out of popular books on contemporary architecture by the mid-1920s. He was the runner-up in a competition to rebuild a well-known school in Preston, Lancashire, in 1919: the winning scheme, by Stanley Adshead, a Regency-style architect then on the way up, looks like a weaker version of Field's own design. And although Lloyds' directors seem to have been happy with Field, he never became "the bank architect," and was never awarded the most prestigious jobs: in fact, his Wealdstone branch of 1903, described in my introduction, marks the high point of his bank-building career. Lloyds' splendid new London headquarters, designed by a large and successful commercial practice, drew closely from Field's own recent design for a branch in Southampton, but no one was on hand to notice it.[5]

Field's early clients had included cabinet ministers and a duke; by the end, tucked away in the picturesque artists' town of Rye in Sussex, he was building small cottages and sheds for widows and a family doctor. In a charming interview for *The Builder* toward the end of his life, he spoke of his youthful admiration for Richard Norman Shaw, who came to a room that he, Field, had designed in a Shavian manner when young. Field then went on to recall that Shaw had been unable to think of anything nice to say about it, a disappointing admission to have to make about one's hero.[6] Nobody knows whether Field fell out with his various associates, or owed his success to them; or was too nice or insufficiently ambitious to develop an assertive, growing practice. Alternatively, for that matter, whether he was too bad-tempered, or difficult to deal with. In fact little seems to be known about his personal and social life beyond his childless marriage to an artist. I have no idea whether Field saw himself as a failure, and for our purposes it does not matter either way. We can all imagine that he heard that epiphonic fanfare, time and time again; and yet nothing substantial, no real fame, no real place in the history books, ever came out of it. A talented and by all accounts decent man, humiliation was all around him, in his life and in posterity.[7]

My impression is that Field was an inspired dreamer: he wanted to convert the pretty imagery of an idealized, mainly early-eighteenth-century English village life, the kind that had been illustrated in his teenage years by Kate Greenaway and Randolph Caldecott, into a reality he could love. He himself was evidently an enthusiastic golfer, and he designed golf pavilions and plenty of houses around golf courses for weekend players. He built himself a cottage just south of the golf course at Woking in Surrey, and Lawrence Weaver's *Small Country Houses of To-day* described the sense of sentiment, prettiness, and retreat that he created there, describing how, on the lintel above the front door opposite a pretty rose garden, Field's favorite sculptor Eric Aumonier "has carved amid a trail of conventional leaves the pious legend: Enter, dear Lord, mine house with me / Until I enter Thine with Thee."[8]

But Field's attempts at re-creating an ideal rural or suburban life were usually hampered. Architecture requires patrons with money and commitment. In Field's case, the members of Lloyds Premises Committee would not let him go any further: they prevented him, for example, from designing picturesque gardens to two of the branches that he built. But I think his talent seemed to have failed him too, and he had no new ideas; the economic situation after the First World War made it very difficult for an old-fashioned, second-rate designer to attract ambitious clients. His later projects almost parody the idiosyncrasies of his earlier ones, with grossly inflated doorcases and consoles. And—perhaps most devastatingly—there is not a single canonical history of Western, or British, or English architecture that has anything to say at all about Field's various genres, even though examples of them are on every British high street; these histories are written by a different sort of person, the kind of person for whom the sentimental or romantic architecture of the beginning of the twentieth century remains a sideshow. Indeed, the Buckinghamshire volume of the "Pevsner" *Buildings of England* series—the most authoritative architectural guide in England, the first point of reference for every serious architectural historian—fails to mention that the branch of Lloyds Bank in the town of Aylesbury is by Field, even though it is the largest and most impressive neoclassical building there.[9]

It is the variety of failure in Field's career that makes him interesting. If we were writing here about the successful designer of some baroque offices and some influential bank branches, we could easily write a two-paragraph footnote to a chapter on neoclassical architecture. But when the true extent of Field's disasters are known, from the sheer impossibility of realizing his old-fashioned village idyll in industrial late-Victorian England, to the decline in his powers, to the seedy, sad nature of some of his forlorn surviving buildings—in the case of his lovely bank branch at Wealdstone, its ravished beauty surrounded by all the ugliness of an uncared-for high street is an almost unbearable sight—the story is suddenly a great deal broader, a great deal more interesting, and says much more about the architect's world than would the very limited conventional story of his few successes.

DIFFERENT TYPES OF LOSER-ARCHITECT

Do we all have something of Horace Field within us? There must surely be elements in the long list of his failures that overlap with ours.

In his book *La noblesse des vaincus*, Jean-Marie Rouart defined 44 figures from Western cultural history as specifically different types of loser
placed in self-explanatory subgroups: *Les désenchantés de l'amour*, *Les
rêveurs de pouvoir*, *Les violonistes de l'autodestruction*, and so on.[10] Each
character then receives a losing epithet of his own: from *Un sado-maso
de l'amour* (Alfred de Musset, most of whose life was blighted by a
hopeless passion for George Sand) to *L'alpiniste du non-sens* (Georges
Perec, whose experimental writing was so abstruse as to lead to his
rejection). Rouart's introduction makes it clear that he finds these losers
much more interesting than the winners, not least because their experiences make them much more like us: *Les vaincus de la vie. Quel écrivain
n'est pas de la famille?* (Life's losers. What writer is not kin to them?) he
asks at the end of his introduction. As usual, critics in the other arts are
somewhere in advance of those who write about architecture. By
searching out and categorizing different types of loser, Rouart intended
to demonstrate how deeply into the consciousness of the ordinary individual a great artist can come. Yet the interesting thing about his selection is that none of them is really a failure; they are successes who are
most interesting when they fail. In this sense, which is evidently not
ours, the Italian baroque architect Francesco Borromini was a failure,
and that is how Rudolf and Margot Wittkower described him and
others in *Born under Saturn*. At any rate, architectural losers can likewise be divided into categories which themselves establish the ways in
which we can best appreciate what it was that they achieved; we can
work out what battles they thought they were fighting and how it is
that we can go about discovering what is challenging, interesting,
moving, elegant, and beautiful in their architecture.

DEATH BY WRIGHT

For me, the whole practice of architecture resounds with failure, to the
extent that I can see an entire unwritten culture of failure about it. The
plot of the East German film *Die Architekten* (The Architects) focuses
on a group of designers who invest all their energies in an imaginative
scheme for a new cultural center on a housing estate, and the failure of
the scheme to gain official approval over the course of a lengthy and

wearying process provides not just a metaphor for the futility of professional ambition in the German Democratic Republic but also the cata-
lyst for the personal breakdown of the members of the team.[11] In fact it
is possibly true that all architectural practice is a failure or an unwin-
nable compromise of some kind: that is certainly what the British critic
Jeremy Till seems to think.[12] In his book *Architects: The Noted and the
Ignored* (1984), Niels L. Prak listed some of the ways in which architects as a profession are on the retreat: they are continually losing professional ground to consultants of various kinds; their relationship with
commercial and speculative builders pushes them away from creativity;
not only are they fenced into carrying out certain specific and limiting
types of work, they are also the victims of a process which forces them
further and further one side or the other of a line which distinguishes
creative artists from mere producers.[13] Architectural competitions
create huge numbers of losers, sometimes losers who fail time and time
again, perhaps only by narrow margins: the endless dashing of dreams.
Every one of these people has lost time, energy, nerves, ambition,
money, and of course pride: pride to their spouses and partners, to
their children, perhaps to their parents, to the more successful architects in their circle of family and friends, to their rivals, to their bank
managers. The corrupt practices of nineteenth-century competitions
caused continuing strain and distress to some people—it was thought
in 1835 that this was what actually killed the British architect Francis
Goodwin, who invested a great deal in competition entries, and was at
the time planning to outdo even his usual high standards in the Houses
of Parliament competition: he died of apoplexy.[14]

Aside from the pessimism of critics, it is clearly true that even rich,
famous, prolific architects never quite get over that one competition
loss that meant so much to them. Field was at least prolific, and far
worse happened to other people. There are architects who are known
only because, paradoxically, their whole existence has been wiped out:
that is the interesting thing about them. Mostly these are people who
got involved with someone famous who went on to denigrate or
patronize them. Frank Lloyd Wright supplies a fine example: his best
friend when he started work was a young architect called Cecil Corwin.

Wright's annihilation of Corwin is described in the *Autobiography*.
It was Corwin—"the fine-looking, cultured fellow with pompadour

and beard"—who greeted Wright when he arrived for his interview with Joseph Silsbee in 1887. As Wright describes it, Corwin not only secured him a job but immediately went out of his way to charm him; he took him out to lunch, lent him ten dollars, and invited him to stay with his family, all on the day of their first meeting.[15] They quickly became inseparable, says Wright; they talked all night, about architecture, religion, everything. They fell out badly only when Wright found himself a girlfriend. Corwin is temporarily forgotten in the narrative while Wright works for Adler and Sullivan—the personal part of the story here is mostly taken up with Wright scrapping with the Jews in the office and working himself into Sullivan's confidence. But then, when Wright started out in practice on his own, Corwin joined him.

Not for long. It is the termination of this deep friendship and professional partnership that is so devastating. Wright became too busy to notice that Corwin was losing interest in his work. Then one day came the extraordinary revelation that Corwin had become so crushed by Wright's genius that he had no heart left for designing anything himself. When Wright finally realized that something was the matter, and asked why, Corwin declared:

> I've found out there's no joy in architecture for me except as I see you do it. It bores me when I try to do it myself. There's the truth for you. You *are* the thing you do. I'm not and I never will be.

The denouement of this awful scene arrives as Corwin wails

> I'm no architect. I know it now.

and flounces off "East." Wright then concluded all reference to the deepest friendship of his life with the comment "Cecil went East and—God knows why—never have I seen him since."[16]

Corwin's only mistake as far as posterity is concerned was to have been in the wrong place at the wrong time, standing beside one of the greatest talents of America; almost everything that his story tells us is actually about Wright and not about him. There are other ways in which the conjunction of the average with the great adds a pathetic character to an architect's reputation, and Wright himself was so

assertive a figure that he seems to have encouraged it—indeed, John
Lautner thought that he himself was one of only a couple of the
Taliesin "apprentices" who ever escaped Wright's shadow, which fell
on them as much in the form of emotional blackmail as of grandiose
bluster.[17] According to Mosette Broderick, who noticed it at first hand
when working with Adolf Placzek at the Avery Architectural Library
at Columbia University in the 1970s, Wright's son John used to buy up
sheets of the 2-cent postage stamp that had his father's face on so that
he could make up larger values for the parcels he posted to the library,
knowing that row upon row of images of the threatening old face
would be canceled out by a plethora of thick black postmarks.

The unasked-for problem that the sons or parents of the famous
have is that the less talented relations are always compared unfavorably
with the latter rather than with anyone of similar talent to themselves.
The great Charles Cockerell was the son of an undistinguished architect
called Samuel Pepys Cockerell, destined to be known almost only as the
architect of a house that was a one-liner—the exotic, Indianesque Sez-
incote in Gloucestershire. Samuel Pepys Cockerell's office employed,
admittedly, Benjamin Latrobe, but also some no-hopers: one was
Joseph Kay, who built dull houses in London. I came across Kay when I
found his unremarkable, and nastily drawn, design for a parsonage
house at Boxworth in Cambridgeshire (1840). So poor Kay's place in
history is as the untalented pupil of the second-rate father of a great
one, a more interesting story than the one about the person who
designed an uninteresting parsonage. A century later, Lutyens's son
Robert was an unremarkable architect who never settled down in any
way, privately or professionally: he annoyed his parents by "designing
sybaritic bathrooms and cocktail bars and furniture," and it seems
unlikely that the buildings credited jointly to his father and himself
actually owed anything to him personally; in addition he was a loser
compared to his successful sisters, the novelist Mary and the composer
Elizabeth.[18] Consequently, the interesting thing about any of Robert's
buildings is how they struggle with those of his father's reputation, of
which they seem to be slight imitations, not their "success" as designs.
What about all the sons of the great Charles Barry, architect and co-
designer with Augustus Pugin of the Palace of Westminster—what did
they actually achieve? Charles Barry junior had a reasonable career, but

an obituary damned him with the deadly phrase "with him the artist was subservient to the man of business," the architecture critic's way of saying that their victim was no good as a designer. Edward Barry built a magnificent opera house in Valletta, the capital of Malta, but it was bombed during the Second World War and has been a ruin ever since; his hotel building at Charing Cross station survives but is the dreariest of the Victorian London train stations, and is now substantially mutilated along its front elevation after bomb damage. George Gilbert Scott's son George junior was a finer designer than his father, but his best building—the church of St. Agnes, Kennington, in south London—was damaged during an air raid in 1941 and then gratuitously demolished, to be replaced by a disappointing cheap shed of a church, so no one can appreciate it anymore; and he himself became mad, was certified insane in 1884 and later died in his father's magnificent Midland Grand Hotel at St. Pancras station in London.[19]

FIGURE 1.1
St. Agnes' Church, Kennington, London, designed by George Gilbert Scott Junior in 1874, as reproduced in *The Architect*, November 16, 1888. Courtesy of Gavin Stamp.

FIGURE 1.2
The replacement church on the same site, designed by Covell &
Matthews in 1956. Courtesy of Keith Diplock.

MORE LOSERS

What architectural tragedies these London railway station hotels have
seen. Edward Welby Pugin, son of Augustus and a designer of ornate,
idiosyncratic French-Gothic buildings, died in the Turkish baths of the
Grosvenor Hotel at Victoria Station in London. He was 40 years old,
as his father had been at the time of his death, but whereas it is now
thought that the women-loving and uxorious Augustus died directly or
indirectly from syphilis, Edward at the same age was a bachelor; a loner;
bitter and bankrupt.[20] Nearly all his unusual domestic architecture has
been destroyed; much of his ecclesiastical work was mutilated by mod-
ernization following the liturgical changes introduced by the Second
Vatican Council: emptied out; whitewashed; refurnished with tat;
retiled (with tiles "similar to those often found in public lavatories," says
the Edward Pugin scholar Gerard Hyland, of the sanctuary at the
architect's Stanbrook Abbey chapel); desecrated.[21] Yet the surviving
buildings of the Barrys, Scott, and Pugin junior are magnificent if they
are presented as the results of a fine artistic and creative temperament
battling with the heritage of a famous father, charged with frustration,
rather than as second-division Victorian monuments. Once one sees it
like that, one sees too that the stylistic references and experiments in

them—Scott's early adoption of the Queen Anne style, and Pugin's of an aggressive French *flamboyant*—are telling stories about their understanding and experience of their parents.

A further problem for Edward Pugin was that he was impossibly bad-tempered and litigious, and that meant his professional partnerships ended disastrously. A bad temper has been the undoing of many good designers. Maybe some architects remained modest practitioners solely because of their moods or because they became angry, or otherwise annoyed those who could have helped them: it is impossible to know how many great architects we might have had but for their temper. Of John Sydney Brocklesby, an unremarkable architect of pleasant Tudoresque interwar villas in south London, his biographers glumly remarked:

> His tendency to take an extreme stance when faced with opposition was a facet of his personality which came increasingly to the fore in later years.[22]

Berthold Lubetkin had an "explosive temper," at least at home: according to his daughter, who filled a whole book with painful reminiscences, he was rude, cruel, autocratic, and paranoid and held grudges for long periods; his retreat from professional life in the mid-1950s was probably related to his hopeless character.[23] Ernö Goldfinger, admittedly, was also the possessor of a vile temper and yet managed to be a success, but by all accounts he did not suffer from the self-doubt that often plagues the angry. Latrobe fell out with almost everybody. Sigurd Lewerentz was an impossible person, grumpy and stubborn: he was kept afloat with his wife's support, and avoided architectural practice for decades between flouncing off the Woodland cemetery project in Stockholm and the two famous churches he produced at the end of his life that have ensured his reputation. Jørn Utzon was evidently a difficult person to deal with too, with very few projects following the troublesome Sydney Opera House; he built little in Denmark itself beyond two small housing estates and one beautiful church, and that in a small, highly cultured country with very few architectural geniuses for clients to choose between. Andrew Saint's retelling of the Sydney debacle quotes the engineer Jack Zunz's recollections of Utzon:

He left the job, he let down many of his friends and closest allies, he split not only the architectural profession, but also the community as a whole, and he left the project in chaos.[24]

Erich Mendelsohn, a very different sort of architect, suffered from being intolerably arrogant, repelling people throughout his career. Although he was one of the greatest designers of the twentieth century, his career was not only destroyed when he was at the height of his creative powers by the Nazis' purge of Jews, but continually and increasingly damaged and plagued by terrible relations with the people he was confronted by in every place of exile he turned to: staff, friends, architects, journalists and critics, curators, pretty much everyone. Julius Posener, at one point his assistant, tried to soften the blow when he wrote: "I found him authoritarian . . . his person aroused antipathy in us, even a certain contempt . . . and the whole fuss of achievement with which he flattered himself. . . . He was one of the most lovable people I have ever met—and at the same time one of the most unpleasant."[25] He failed to charm his jealous Bauhaus contemporaries while still in Germany, and made long-term enemies of all of them.[26] He became, surely, an angry man, set upon everywhere by the second-rate after his cruel eviction from Germany, where his practice had been the largest and most successful in the country. After a short period in England, where he managed to alienate the influential *Architectural Review*, he sought exile in British Mandate Palestine and quickly fell out with the architects of the Zionist movements because of his arrogance but also, probably, because in their view he collaborated too willingly with the Mandate authorities on public commissions in spite of the fact that he had long been a committed Zionist himself.[27] It is said that his final exile, in America, was poisoned by his having brusquely put the telephone down on Philip Johnson, which caused his omission from the seminal International Style exhibition, and no doubt the fact that his Bauhaus rivals had already established themselves there resulted in the design of scarcely more than a handful of projects in the country before his premature death. It is hard to claim that Mendelsohn was a loser as a conventional architect, because of the recognized greatness of his architecture; yet in many senses he was—not only because of his badly timed or ill-judged and unfulfilled exiles, his personal character and his early death, but also because virtually every significant building of his in Germany (and there were many) was destroyed or mutilated; in fact in the case of one of the greatest of them all, the Schocken store in Stuttgart, this happened well after the Nazi regime, the war and the bombing were over. Of his magnificent Jewish cemetery in Königsberg nothing has survived Kristallnacht and Russian occupation beyond a small fragment—mutilated, reclad, miserable—of its entrance pavilion.

Early demolition or mutilation will blight the reputation of even the best architects. All—*all*—of the innovative interior design work of Wells Coates in London has been destroyed, including his BBC radio studios where his Japanese-Hollywood modernism was brilliantly combined with technological equipment that he, an engineer with a doctorate, had designed and integrated into them.[28] John Martin Robinson's recent monograph on the late Georgian architect James Wyatt explains that one of the problems Wyatt's reputation has faced is that too many of his finest buildings were demolished, or indeed fell down, or caught alight, in some cases only a matter of a few years after they were erected, or sometimes even before they were finished; the Oxford Street Pantheon, in central London, and his astonishing Fonthill Abbey in Wiltshire, with its soaring central tower, would be recognized as two of the great buildings of England had they survived. Wyatt failed to draw and publish his buildings because of his slothfulness, and that in itself deterred or actively repelled those clients who were not disgusted by his behavior with women and drink; and in time all these also ensured that the next generation of architects, the pious and high-minded Gothic Revivalists, despised him more than anyone else.[29]

Yet being nice is not always an asset, and too much money can also be a problem, as, no doubt, can laziness; an obituary writer noted of George Gilbert Scott junior: "The routine and discipline of an architect's office were never to Mr. Scott's taste, and being possessed of ample private means, he gradually withdrew from practice."[30] Surely the same is true of the brilliant Halsey Ricardo, an arts and crafts architect who built the luscious blue-and-green-tiled Debenham House on the fringes of Kensington in 1905–1908; in addition to being "dark, Jewish, spectacularly good-looking, musical and a typical architectural amateur," according to his cousin Harry Goodhart-Rendel, he was also extremely well off.[31] He never designed anything of any significance again. Some people's reputation comes to an end because they seem to lose their talent: M. H. Baillie Scott, the winner of the prestigious international *Haus eines Kunstfreundes* competition in 1901, and the designer of superbly original houses in the late-Victorian and Edwardian era, spent the second half of his career designing (with some difficulty, in the prevalent economic climate) uninteresting half-timbered neo-Tudor homes; as he sank, Mackintosh rose, to the extent that it is the latter's unsuccessful competition scheme that is now remembered. A further British example, following on immediately from Scott's decline, is that of William Crabtree, the supposedly brilliant protégé of the influential Charles Reilly, who had worked for Raymond Hood and Joseph Emberton. Reilly managed to get him adopted as the co-architect of the Mendelsohnesque Peter Jones store in Sloane Square, London, but his architectural reputation has never extended beyond that one building. The "young and gifted" architect, as his obituarist described him, "also designed hospitals, factories and schools in Harlow," thus linking the whole of the rest of his career to undistinguished and unrecognized obscurity in one of the New Towns of the 1950s.[32]

At the same time, being too sophisticated, or too demanding, or too unclassifiable, or too difficult to grasp, can be a problem for architects: it is for this reason, according to the architectural historian and critic Peter Blundell Jones, that two of the leading organic architects of the late twentieth century, Lucien Kroll and Peter Hübner, have never received the acclaim they deserve from critics: they are both "untidy, disordered, threatening anarchy, breaking what is seen as good architectural manners."[33] Perhaps there is an unresolvable paradox in a commitment to organic architecture anyway: if you follow the logic of the argument to the end, you become incomprehensible to too many people, just as you become unassessable by unimaginative critics.

SOCIETIES OF LOSERS

There have been distinct periods when women—all women—have been marked out as losers by the architectural establishment; the professionalization of architecture in the nineteenth century, for example, with the formation of the Institute of British Architects in 1837, seems to have almost completely ended the rare practice by women of the design of buildings. A battle had to be fought at the end of the nineteenth century for their return, but countless talented women did not have the energy to put themselves in the firing line of both family and profession. No doubt there were many such as the Swede Ingrid Wallberg, born in 1890, who were not allowed to enter the profession, who gained their architectural education where they could, and whose significant influence on the work of famous men (in her case, the Gothenburg and Stockholm planner Albert Lilienberg; Le Corbusier, for whom she worked on the Villa Savoye; and Albert Roth) is undocumented and hard to trace.[34] Nowadays most young architects of both sexes still go through a losing period: they can be exploited and bullied by architectural offices that treat these young graduates as draftsmen, so that they find it hard to put together a decent standard of living on their first salary. They may not even be paid, if they are interns in an office that is unscrupulous enough to attract them to work there for nothing. Throughout their careers their work is subsumed, or lost, in the projects that go under the name of their superiors, even once they have become a partner; and even in the case of a well-known building: "The thing with Rodney Gordon is that he couldn't be bothered to publicise himself," Jonathan Meades told Chris Foges of the Brutalist architect admired for the buildings he designed for the Owen Luder Partnership, which in the nature of things are generally linked to Luder's own name and not his own.[35] And of course there will be architects in offices of middle size and upward who never see a building of their own realized, however great their talent for design, decade after decade of hard work buried in frustration and obscurity.

Some other losers come in groups: McKim, Mead and White were surrounded throughout their careers by the loser-architects in their own office, professionals who were losers as people too, right from the beginning; a further aspect of the curse that seemed to descend upon them is the fact that just about all of their finest houses have been demolished; and then Stanford White's personal reputation was forever sullied after he was murdered by a young psychotic. At least one can say that McKim, Mead and White's loser-architects were mostly talented designers—the principal designers of the firm, in fact—but in some cases architects who were powerful personalities seem to have encouraged an entourage of mediocrity. David Watkin points to the example of the office of John Soane, one of England's leading public architects in the early decades of the nineteenth century: they were "not really high achievers as architects," he remarks with understatement.[36] Was this the result of Soane's own paranoia and jealousy? The only good designer Soane employed was George Basevi, whose tragic end has been mentioned; most of them were hopeless, unremembered, or remembered for the wrong reasons, and they compare unfavorably with the ambitious, bright-eyed young men working soon afterward in the offices of George Gilbert Scott senior and George Edmund Street, both hothouses for the talent that characterizes the triumphal era of the Gothic Revival.

Some of those Soane employed exemplify further ways in which an architect can be a loser. James Adams, working there between 1806 and 1809, was a Royal Academy gold medalist, but immediately embarked upon a forgotten career: he was, in other words, an example of the phenomenon that every architecture school teacher knows: the high-scoring student with the wow factor who never makes anything of themselves thereafter. Christopher Webster, an enthusiast for the "lost 1830s," explains in his recent biography that R. D. Chantrell, another Soane pupil, was a supporter of the new correct Gothic style when it exploded in the late 1830s, and even joined the Cambridge Camden Society, its irrepressible, ruthless standard-bearers; but that did not save him from their mockery when he turned out to be no good at doing it himself, and the great Pugin made a special object of ridicule out of his ambitious parish church at Leeds after visiting it: it was a huge, expensive, embarrassing failure.[37] George Wightwick, also a Soane protégé, is in a slightly different category; although he too was no good as a Gothic designer, and was effectively boycotted by the new men and driven into exile in the far-flung counties of southwest England as a result, his reminiscences of Soane have given him a sort of immortality. David Mocatta, sometimes called the first railway architect, is at least remembered for that reason in heritage circles, and also for the design of Moses Montefiore's unexpected and only partially surviving complex of Jewish buildings in the seaside town of Ramsgate, Kent, but never for the quality of his work. But as for Parke,

Papendiek, Mee, Malton, Seward, Underwood, Foxhall—who were they, and what is their memorial?

Edward Cresy, eager and enthusiastic, poured his energy and time into fine sets of measured architectural drawings of Roman and Italian Gothic buildings in the 1820s, but too few people showed an interest, probably because John Britton and others were doing the same thing, only better, and Cresy exiled himself to France. When he returned he became a building inspector, made himself a name as a civil engineer, and thus took himself out of conventional architectural history. His eventual architectural achievements—a house or two, and a square off Knightsbridge—are insignificant and unremarkable, especially when compared to the fine things he had drawn.[38] Worse still was the case of William Railton, who as the author of a premiated scheme for the Houses of Parliament competition, and then as a successful competitor for the design of what became Nelson's Column in Trafalgar Square in 1839, should have been set up for life; he took up a prestigious position as architect to the new Ecclesiastical Commissioners, no doubt expecting a rich career building bishops' palaces as well as countless parsonages, but he was so out of spirit with the new Gothic Revivalists, and his professional and technical abilities were so limited when faced with the rapid changes of his era, that he was bullied or shamed by his employers into abandoning architecture altogether. When he died, nearly thirty years later, he did not even receive the dignity of an obituary in *The Builder*.[39] The more I research it, the more I feel that the architectural rout by the Gothic Revivalists of the 1840s created a wave of losers of astonishing variety and lasting impact.

Then there are designers who were completely out of their depth: this is often true where the technical aspect of a structure is concerned. The building of the Anglican cathedral in Valletta in the 1830s, in any case an inauspicious project in strenuously Catholic Malta, involved a series of architects who seem to have been incapable of doing the job in hand.[40] The first of these was a Lieutenant Colonel Whitmore, whose professional ability was called into question when he failed to include the foundations in his design and estimate for the building in 1825. He was followed as a result by Richard Lanksheer, who began as a cabinetmaker, of all things, to the British in Malta but became Head Superintendent of Civil Artificers in 1830, probably as the result of some political maneuvering. The cathedral became a pet project of Queen Adelaide, wife of William IV, and she laid the foundation stone as queen dowager in March 1839. But Lanksheer's structural design failed—mainly, it seems, because he had no knowledge of building with the local stone. The cathedral building then had to be reconstructed, this time by William Scamp, assistant to the Director of Engineering Works of the Admiralty. Then Scamp's building failed as well; it needed alterations, and during reconstruction works a cornice fell and killed five workmen. Much antagonism followed in the local press, and Scamp was branded as incompetent by the Maltese not least because he was British, some kind of Protestant devil. Here the project itself seemed to suck loser-architects into it, no doubt not that rare a phenomenon.

A leading example of an architect who was not up to it—not only because of his lack of design skills, but also because of the way he became a victim of cost-cutting and battles between politicians—is Ralph Knott, the young winner of a prestigious competition in 1907 to

FIGURE 1.3
The early-nineteenth-century designers of St. Paul's Anglican Cathedral, Valletta, Malta, were all losers. Courtesy of the author.

design the London County Hall, the city's municipal headquarters, on an unequalled prominent site diagonally across the Thames from the Palace of Westminster. Knott's original design was criticized bitterly by unsuccessful competitors—Lutyens, in particular—and all the grandeur and élan that it originally had were forced out of it, bit by bit. He did not live to see its completion—he died "quite suddenly" in 1929, according to a biographer, aged only 50, possibly wrecked by drink. The only other building he designed of any significance was the former Speaker's House at Stormont, the legislative assembly of Northern Ireland, but Wikipedia currently pays Knott a final insult by telling you that this was the work of the arch-winner, Lutyens. For a new line of loserdom has opened up recently as a result of the rapid broadcast of incorrect information on the web that soon finds itself embedded into journalism and a thousand (or more) student essays, in this case a work by one lesser-known architect being attributed to another one who was already better known, with no real means of defense or correction.

FIGURE 1.4
The compromised design and prolonged building of County Hall, built as the seat of London's government, turned its architect Ralph Knott into a loser. Courtesy of Keith Diplock.

MUTILATION, FRUSTRATION, AND DEATH

Then there are people who are remembered mainly because they mutilated or extended a good building by a better architect. Mendelsohn designed a fine villa for the Schocken family in Jerusalem, but it was wrecked in the 1950s by Josef Klarwein when he turned it into a music academy. In fact Klarwein, who had worked before his enforced exile from Germany as a senior assistant of Fritz Höger, turned out to be perhaps Israel's greatest loser. He was one of the finest architects working in the state during its early years, in a dry but careful and always beautifully detailed style; but after winning the competition for the new Knesset building in 1957 he fell victim to a fate similar to that of Gepstein, only a great deal worse. The fashionable young architects of the Labor movement fell upon him; the job was taken from him by stealth; and his reputation was comprehensively rubbished for the rest of his life.[41] He was—in private, at any rate—even described as a "Nazi" by at least one of his detractors for the Germanic and un-Middle Eastern pains he took with the planning and the detailing of his buildings.[42]

In England one of the most prominent examples of mutilation-loserdom is that of Thomas Robinson, the otherwise forgotten designer of the plain, uninteresting Palladian wing at Vanbrugh's magnificently baroque Castle Howard in Yorkshire, an extension that required the demolition of Vanbrugh's "great cabinet."[43] So pleased was Robinson with his work that he wanted to demolish the other wing of Vanbrugh's house to put up another dull block of his own. Another form of ensuring eternal notoriety is to add an unnecessary addition to a fine building: remaining for a moment longer at Castle Howard, one can see this in the silly steps added to Hawksmoor's noble mausoleum by one Daniel Garrett, another of the Palladian Lord Burlington's useless protégés.[44] An architectural story about either of these two should be about anything other than what conventional architectural history might expect from them.

Alongside the mutilators are the loser-architects who built over the ruins of fine buildings that were destroyed to accommodate them: we have seen the case of Herbert Baker, hopelessly trying to defend the almost indefensible act of being party to the destruction of Soane's

Bank of England and then trying to disguise it. The architects of the building that replaced Penn Station in New York—and their British equivalent, the Architects Department of the British Railways Board, who put up the unloved structure that replaced Thomas Hardwick's famous propylaeum at Euston, one of London's main train stations—are obvious examples. Offensive too are the architects who designed a disappointing building because the original highly regarded one never came off; my own childhood town center of Hammersmith is now blighted by a monstrously ugly office and transportation hub in a clumsy postmodern style designed by Elsom Pack & Roberts, who put it up when an elegant proposal by Foster Associates never materialized. A more famous example is Liverpool Metropolitan Cathedral, of which the architect was the affable Frederick Gibberd, on the losing side in the prolonged tasteless and acrimonious battle between British Brutalists (who won) and Scandinavianists (who lost, at least until recently).[45] For many, however, Gibberd's major crime is that his building went up on top of the only small fragment of Lutyens's fantastically ambitious original design for the building, a failure that ought to be Lutyens's, or the Catholic hierarchy's, but which somehow seems to be attached unfairly to Gibberd.

And then there is the tragedy of the great building left unbuilt, or the unsatisfactory version of it that an architect was forced to put up instead. Many architects have a great "unbuilt": for Shaw in 1864 it was the Bradford Exchange; for Lutyens in 1907 it was the London County Hall. My cousin Leonard Manasseh, influential tutor to a decade of students at the Architectural Association in the 1950s, designed a new law courts building for the city of Bath in the early 1970s. It was to be the great pinnacle of his career, a Corbusian temple that reconciled the Georgian city with the twentieth century; but its realization was frustrated by a combination of public opposition to further new development in the city, and new guidelines on secure design following a bomb attack in London by the Irish Republican Army. He poured his frustration into the next project to come up, and the only memorial now to his grand idea is a small temple-like pumping station near the Dorset coast, recently defaced by the local council's idea of art—that is, the daubing of its walls with "murals."[46]

Of the miseries of architects in exile there is plenty more yet to be said: Mendelsohn at least continued to attract critical acclaim. Myra Wahrhaftig dedicated much of her life before her untimely death to describing what happened to refugees from Nazism who ended up in British Mandate Palestine: a characteristically awful story is that of the distinguished theater architect Oskar Kaufmann, who was driven out of his smart Schöneberg flat in Berlin to a poky room in Tel Aviv; who failed to find work; who almost starved; who was then commissioned to design a major theater in Tel Aviv, which was never finished, and which now, having been mutilated by other architects over several decades, has vanished altogether under a slick, characterless façade.[47] Kaufmann himself gave up in despair at conditions in Tel Aviv and went on to Budapest to face further persecution.[48] Among the dead there must surely have been countless geniuses. Among the wounded and the damaged there must have been many who had been forced to abandon their dream of becoming an architect.

FIGURE 1.5
Oskar Kaufmann's modest apartment block in Yael Street, Tel Aviv, is a testament to his unhappy career in the city. Courtesy of the author.

But death also afflicts the known and the promising in secure, peaceful countries. AIDS and other conditions that were once terminal will have taken with them countless architect-victims, and obscured the records of those who had achieved wonderful things before their death. Some names will live on only so long as there are firsthand witnesses to remember them. One is that of Edward Reynolds, an outstanding student who joined the fourth year at the AA in 1956 after working on, and contributing to the design of, the Brutalist Alton West estate at Roehampton, southwest London, under Bill Howell. Reynolds died "after a long and painful illness" at the age of 32 on January 1, 1959, his memory surviving in the record of his remarkable Scharounian student scheme (with A. Lee) for a concert hall in Trafalgar Square, and in the minds of those such as James Gowan who studied or worked with him.[49] There are also accidents. Maciej "Matthew" Nowicki, the Polish-born modernist, pioneer of the hyperbolic paraboloid and a promising talent, was killed in an airplane crash in 1950 on his way back from a visit to the site of the new Indian city of Chandigarh, where he was intended to be the master planner; the job went instead to Le Corbusier, and to Fry and Drew, all hard, determined, winning people, and Nowicki became a posthumous loser. Something similar happened, but at an earlier stage of life, with Michael Ventris, a distinguished young archaeologist as well as architect in London. He was killed in a road accident at 34, a fact that has made his small, unpretentious house in Hampstead far more intriguing than the contemporary one by the successful architect Kenneth Capon on the other side of the road from it, even though there is not really any significant difference in quality or style between the architecture of the two of them—a tangible example of exactly how failure can be more interesting than success. Old age and reputation are no protection either; in the 1980s lawyers discovered that British architects were almost completely unprotected against professional negligence claims, even spurious or gratuitous ones, and set about assaulting them. One of the most shocking cases to emerge was that of 89-year-old Bertram Carter, the former secretary of the MARS group who had trained with the great Lutyens (who, along with E. Beresford Pite, signed his Royal Institute of British Architects nomination papers), and whose streamlined flats in Richmond, to the southwest of London, were published in 1935 in

FIGURE 1.6
The fame of Michael Ventris's unremarkable house in Hampstead,
north London, is mainly due to his early death. Courtesy of Keith
Diplock.

the *Architects' Journal* alongside Lutyens's Midland Bank in Manchester; he was, said the London *Times*, "a man of great integrity." The stress of being pursued by lawyers for a job completed many years before he had retired a decade earlier eventually killed him.[50]

ARCHITECTS EAT ARCHITECTS

The epiphonic music I listened to when I was a student came in the form of wistful ballads by the English singer Peter Skellern; what I loved about his songs was that they were sometimes prefaced by a short but splendid burst of grand brass-band music, a terrific fanfare of some kind, which was then followed bathetically by lyrics about some lonely or lovelorn teenager in a miserable industrial town in Lancashire, dreaming of something better and unlikely to get it for a while. They were camp, and they were sentimental. It has been said of Skellern, as it has of other gentle and humorous balladeers of the period, that their careers were thrown off course in the late 1970s by the arrival of the ugly phenomenon of punk, which, while it might have been aimed as an attack on the bubble-gum music of the large record companies,

actually brought down other singer-songwriters instead; certainly the latter almost never made it afterward into what was then called the hit parade.

Like devours like: musicians devour musicians, architects devour architects. Architects are continually under attack from all sides outside their profession—not just from lawyers, builders, developers, and unforgiving clients, but also from supposed friends: biographers can bully architects and their reputations, with entirely irrelevant information about their health or their predilections somehow entering the public consciousness; and even sociologists, not generally assertive people, can bully too, by claiming that the purpose of a building is for something other than to house and delight, or impress, or enrich: for them it is to do with providing a service to whichever section of the population they happen to have taken an interest in recently. Everyone can bully architects in one way or another: and yet if there is one theme that emerges clearly behind nearly all the cases above it is that no one can bully an architect more, no one can be more responsible for turning an architect into a loser, than the other architects and the critics who decide whether your building is a "success"; whether it is "real" or "fake"; "good" or "no good"; whether you deserve a second chance or not: and all on the basis of lines of engagement that were drawn up nearly 200 years ago and never seem to have changed.

2

THERE IS REAL AND THERE IS FAKE

WHO WILL RESCUE THE UNLOVED BUILDINGS?

Sometimes I think I am surrounded by architectural failures. They seem to jump out at me from everywhere, and if it wasn't enough that some or maybe most architects are dismissed as losers, some buildings never had a hope of being taken seriously either. Driving through the ancient Norfolk market town of Swaffham the other day, I came across two losers facing each other across Station Street. On the left, the western side, was the Baptist church, a mean-looking yellow-brick building that had evidently been designed at a point in the mid-nine-teenth century when its style—cheap, slightly incompetent classical—was at its least fashionable. On the other side of the road was the Catholic church. This was about a hundred years more recent, in brown-red brick and vaguely late-medieval or Tudor in style with tall gables and buttresses, but also, oddly, with round-headed windows and what looked like quoins. The Baptist church sat directly on the pavement, but the Catholic one was lost in an ugly parking lot. These two buildings were intended in the first case for a minority sect and in the second for a church which, traditionally, was regarded with suspi-cion in Norfolk and East Anglia, a center of evangelical religion. It was perhaps appropriate, then, that the styles in which they were designed have been written out of architectural histories. All this was instantly clear from flashing by in a car at 30 miles per hour.

When I got back to the library I looked them up in the *Buildings of England*, the "Pevsner" guides which, in their recent editions, generally

include even small and unremarkable suburban churches. The guide
introduces the yellow-brick building as follows:

> Further N the terrible BAPTIST CHURCH, built in 1858,
> yellow brick, all round arched, and with two tall corner towers
> with Italianate roofs. The interior is more pleasant. A gallery on
> two sides, sweeping round at the E (entrance) side on twisted
> cast-iron pillars. Fittings all intact including a marble total-
> immersion font.

It goes on to say:

> On the E side of Station Street less of interest.[1]

And with that the guide condemns the Catholic church, which is not
mentioned at all, to critical oblivion. When I later looked up its website I discovered that its dedication is to Our Lady of Pity; at the top of
the site's homepage there is a tiny photograph of Oxburgh Hall, a local
building with Catholic connections. Oxburgh is a large and picturesque late-medieval house—in fact, one of the buildings I had come to
Norfolk to visit—and it owes its current appearance almost entirely to
the early-nineteenth-century passion for Tudor architecture expressed
through the work of J. C. Buckler and, possibly, also of that great
winner Augustus Pugin: something of a sad contrast with a little
almost-Tudor Catholic church marooned on an ugly suburban site.[2]
The image I formed in my mind, therefore, was of the church's architect (let us say it was a man, as it probably was) dreaming of creating a
masterpiece of Tudor architecture, but knowing that his cheap little
building, unlikely to be a masterpiece even in his own eyes, was never
going to get him there.

What a spectacle of unfolding tragedy, then, from these two or
three seconds in the car. A series of potential disasters opens up at
once. There is a story about why these architects chose these ambitious
styles for their buildings, and together with that there is another one
about how the buildings themselves relate to the great styles of the
past. Then there is the fact that one is dismissed as "terrible" by the
country's authoritative guide, and the other one ignored entirely. In

addition, their designers were possibly deluding themselves that they were good at what they were doing—claiming, as it were, that the pale lilac heather was white—or, worse still, were well aware that they were not. The vision of a kind of tragic architectural waste which these churches present is an affecting one, yet buildings like these form the majority of structures in every town. It therefore came as something of a relief when I later discovered that Our Lady of Pity turned out to have been designed by the parish priest himself, without the help of any professional architect.[3]

But, most importantly, these buildings never had a chance in the first place. There is a reason why some buildings never appear on the critics' radar. Whole divisions of architectural style have never been through a process of intelligent criticism or debate. The awkward high-Victorian provincial-classical and the cheap mid-twentieth-century almost-Tudor are firmly in that category. It is not surprising, therefore, that the results are not very good: indeed, the buildings are clumsy, incompetently derivative, badly judged. The same is true of almost all new homes built today that have adopted some kind of washed-out, cheap and unhistorical version of a traditional style, and indeed is even more so where the designers have consciously tried to avoid any historical reference altogether, as if they themselves knew any better than everything history has brought them. In the area where I live—and, no doubt, not far from you too—a whole neighborhood has recently been erected in a nonstyle of white rendered walls, flat or pointlessly wavy roofs in colored metal, plastic window frames, and cheaply applied vertical timber boarding. If anyone unsympathetic were to look at them, they would conclude that their designers were third-rate, and that their buildings were below the critical radar, as the "Pevsner" guide did of the Catholic church. And yet it is not *their fault*. It is lack of a reasonable conversation about architecture, a conversation which is also about life and its experiences, that has turned these buildings into failures and their designers into losers.

We recognize that most people, whoever they are, even those who are completely uninterested in architecture, generally appreciate plain Georgian-type row houses, even where these are not particularly distinguished. A clumsy row of eighteenth-century houses with some vernacular idiosyncrasy to it is often described as charming—for example, the central pavilions of the early-nineteenth-century terraces at New Square, Cambridge, which are divided into an even, rather than odd, number of major bays, so that a pilaster inelegantly descends from the middle of the base of the pediment. Georgian houses and the simplified version of classical architecture associated with them developed very slowly and carefully in order for otherwise uneducated builders to be able to erect them; they were also derived, at least in their details, from examples which were widely circulated and published, and originated in the work of first-rate designers. The London Building Act of 1774, which determined the precise pattern of London row houses, was drafted by no less capable a pair of architects than Robert Taylor and George Dance the Younger, already the architects, respectively, of the Bank of England and Newgate Prison. Houses of this type have been the subject of considerable scholarly debate for over a hundred years in all the countries that saw their construction. The style was defined, discussed, analyzed. It is relatively easy to appreciate what works about them and what does not. But no one has had anything positive to say about the styles of our two victims, the two Norfolk churches, and the styles they were based on, for a very long time indeed. If there is no debate and no discussion, then there is no development and no perfection. The people who created them wanted to conjure up a set of images and associations when they designed their churches, but nobody much was listening, and there was no person or means to help them and put them right, or to develop their style. And there is almost nothing in the language of current architectural criticism that would have helped them today.

Contemporary architects working in traditional styles have had this problem in the past, particularly while modernism was still largely unchallenged. From the mid-1950s and up to the mid-1990s, the classical-Georgian style was abandoned almost altogether, and the thread was broken, at least among practitioners. Reviewing a large neo-Georgian scheme for offices in 1988 by the neoclassical architect Quinlan Terry, for a prominent riverside site in the center of Richmond, the picturesque and historic village on the edges of Greater London, Peter Blundell Jones wrote:

> The tragedy with Terry is that he is unable to reinterpret. . . . He is not working in a living tradition and so cannot enjoy the corrective influence of colleagues.[4]

And that, I think, is exactly right. Nothing affected postwar historical building more than the fact that there was, for about forty years, no intelligent conversation about it. And then a deluge of traditional housing arrived, probably encouraged by the fact that buyers at the top end of the market seemed to prefer it, but also by a new attitude to design by town planners who had grown up among the civic devastation of the 1960s. British architecture students will tell you that a new house should look "contemporary," that is, white and vaguely modernistic, even though most contemporary housing in Britain is actually designed in incompetent versions of historical styles, an example of the dimness of debate that I am struck by as year follows year.

There is one striking and successful example of an organized attempt to create a debate around a debased architectural style in order to revive it. In 1974 the planning department of the county of Essex, to the immediate northeast of London, published a design guide to encourage developers to come up with buildings that would be supported at the planning permission stage. This came as a response to the postwar years of charmless, characterless housing, set in ugly roads, that had come to Essex as it had to everywhere else. The authors of the design guide identified some characteristics of traditional vernacular housing in the county—the angles of gables, the proportions of windows, the walling materials, and so on—and encouraged them, along with the design of new road layouts to create better-thought-out, denser, and frankly more picturesque streets. The design guide was applied: a village called South Woodham Ferrers was greatly expanded on its basis; over time it has been revised and reissued. It was the architectural forerunner of the design guides and manifestos of American New Urbanism, about which more later. And it achieved its aim, which was to force house-builders, whether architects or not, to think more clearly about how they had handled the elements of vernacular architecture.[5] Needless to say, the *Essex Design Guide* was treated with derision by architecture critics writing in the professional press, and it became a byword for everything they disapproved of: folksiness; pastiche; sentimentality. And thus the Essex style, in spite of its evident success in its own terms, became a victim of an architectural hate campaign aimed at a specific way of designing.

There is a distinct pattern to the types of buildings that are approved or disapproved of by architectural historians—and it is striking, too, that these rules of taste have been applied consistently for about 200 years. The fault of the Swaffham Catholic church is that it is in a variant of the Tudor style, a cheap one reduced to a series of small details: the way the parapet continues horizontally at the base of the porch gable; the brickiness, and fussiness in the buttresses; even, perhaps, to stretch a point, the fact that round-headed windows have been incorporated incongruously into its design in the same way that Elizabethan architects began to insert clumsy borrowings from early neoclassical architecture into theirs. In the 1950s, when this church went up, this style would have been a bad choice for an ambitious architect because, for some reason, the late-Tudor architecture which sat somewhere at the bottom of the inspiration for this mean and cheap building had long been the one for which high-art designers had traditionally more contempt than for any other, excepting only a brief period around the turn of the last century when it made a respectable appearance as one of a number of devices employed by arts and crafts architects.

ALL CRITICS HATE TUDOR ARCHITECTURE

There is no particularly logical reason why this should be. Tudor architecture, from the late-medieval version of it around at the time of Henry VII's accession in 1485 right through to the early seventeenth century, has a great deal to be said for it, not only in terms of its beauty and originality but also of the role it could play, as much as any other expression of historical building, in the story of the development of some of the best modern and contemporary architecture—even by the criteria of the modernists themselves. The same may well be true of much northern European half-timbered architecture of the same period. To give one simple example: some surviving sixteenth-century houses were built in the form of a modular skeleton timber frame that allowed continuous strip windows to occupy the whole of an elevation. Little Moreton Hall, the well-known manor house in Cheshire, is like this, but so were countless others, even in towns: there is a fine one in Preston, Lancashire, that survived long enough to be recorded in 1836 in a book by the architect Matthew Habershon (bad-tempered—probably his undoing; a loser, and probably a failure; involved with the design of the original Anglican cathedral in Jerusalem, a project marred by professional disaster), illustrated by a teenage artist called Ewan Christian who went on to be one of the most respected and prolific church and diocesan architects in England.[6] Habershon was a lover of Elizabethan architecture, yet he made no comment about the potential of this approach to contemporary design; neither did anyone else. No one who wrote about the importance of function, or the logic or potential of a structural frame, even once as far as I can see, noted that the Elizabethans had been here before. Elizabethan architects could do symbolic geometry as well as anybody, and they could construct using and expressing the natural properties of materials. All of this is now right in front of our eyes, and the architectural historian Mark Girouard has written the first full and thorough illustrated history of it.[7] It would be perfectly possible—logical, rational, sensible, even teleological, if that is what you are looking for—to describe the history of much mid-

FIGURE 2.1
An old house in Preston, Lancashire, from Matthew Habershon's *Ancient Half-Timbered Houses of England* (1836–1839): strip windows on a loadbearing modular frame about 300 years before the Bauhaus.

twentieth-century modern architecture in terms of its development from these Tudor paradigms. But of course nobody does.

The 1820s and 1830s saw a modest Tudor-Elizabethan revival in England. Some good books were published, and some charming and significant houses built, especially those by the country house architect Anthony Salvin. But for some reason the Tudor style attracted a level of opprobrium from England's most ambitious architects that was quite unprecedented; and the idea was born that a style could constitute some kind of enemy that must be destroyed. Pugin considered Queen Elizabeth herself to be a "female demon," and said nothing further about the buildings of her reign.[8] Alfred Bartholomew—like Pugin attempting to revive architecture on the basis of effective construction—dedicated a chapter of his book *Specifications* to "The Gross Corruption of the Kind of Building called 'Elizabethan'," a style which, he went on to say, was founded in "ignorance and corruption":[9]

> Indeed it would seem, that Gothic architecture having continued in purity longer in England than in any other country, in revenge, building all at once broke up in design, in execution, and in science, and fell here suddenly to a degree of corruption lower than in any country.[10]

The style was like

> a book with its morals reversed by negatives, its sentences misplaced, its words misspelt, its grammar corrupted, some of the words left in English, the remainder translated into different foreign languages, and the whole badly printed upon bad paper.[11]

Two years later the widely read encyclopedist Joseph Gwilt, by and large liberal in his views and well disposed to different English historical styles, had caught up with the latest fashion for dismissal and described Elizabethan architecture as the "imperfectly understood adaption of classic forms to the habits of its day in this country . . . full of redundant and unnerving ornament."[12] And so they went on.

Much neo-Tudor and neo-Elizabethan architecture of their period was indeed incompetent. Yet some was original and memorable—for example, the small number of houses that struggled to combine both neoclassical and neo-Tudor ideas, perhaps adopting the overall form of the latter but the detailing of the former, or vice versa. While researching the forgotten domestic architecture of the 1830s, in the no-man's-land between the end of neoclassicism and the beginning of the Gothic Revival, I discovered not only houses like these, but also poignant little ones that, in an affecting way, appeared to be half "Georgian" and half "Gothic," rather as if they were transgendered buildings, making their way from one identity to another.[13] It seems that the domestic architecture of the 1830s, as it segues between styles, with the rapid application of new building technologies and the vast amount of writing on house-building that were suddenly available, has simply been too complicated for rational discussion by conventional architectural historians, and when I came to write about this period I found that no one had done so before.[14] In many ways this is a fascinating era in English architecture. But the critics, and the architects, and the bullies of the Gothic Revival closed down the discussion and killed the neo-Tudor for some thirty years, until it was temporarily and gloriously revived by George Devey and, especially, Norman Shaw in the 1860s, even if the latter's use of "fake" half-timbering when building in the Tudor style has posed a problem for his admirers.[15]

The general public are not as stupid as architecture critics. One of the major cultural phenomena of the early nineteenth century, beautifully recorded by Peter Mandler in the opening chapter of his book *The Fall and Rise of the Stately Home* but in general familiar to anyone who has ever studied Sir Walter Scott, is the fact that during this period a fascination for Tudor and Elizabethan architecture seized the imagination of pretty much everyone who could read and write in England.[16] Scott himself, after the publication of *Kenilworth* in 1821, provided most of the inspiration for this, and his writing and that of his imitators brought us the first multimedia cultural experiences: a story that began as a novel was soon transformed into popular prints and paintings, exhibitions, theatrical performances, dances, revels, and much else—all the things that people enjoy. Another contributor to this movement was the artist Joseph Nash, a former pupil of A. C. Pugin, whose series of plates entitled *The Mansions of England in the Olden Time* propagated an image of a happy, contented, well-fed land, romantic and picturesque, where servants ate and reveled with their masters, where a fire was blazing, and where maidens sat demurely and poets sang. The imagery was new, but the idea that many people looked for tranquility, joy, comfort, nostalgia and well-being in their architecture as much as in their lives had been evident for a long time in other types of writing about architecture: for example in John Carter's articles in the *Gentleman's Magazine* from the late 1790s; in book reviews in the *Quarterly Review*; in J. C. Loudon's widely circulated journalism and *Encyclopaedia* of 1833; and anywhere else at the time where people discussed Tudor or Gothic architecture as the embodiment of memory or history.

In the early twentieth century, as the arts and crafts movement became transformed from a young men's crusade to a nostalgic move-ment, writers returned to this theme in popular and illustrated books, for example the many that emerged from Batsford, the popular pub-lishers on architecture for a general readership. In 1908, in a book called *The Charm of the English Village*, P. H. Ditchfield fell into a series of raptures about late-medieval and Tudor houses:

> But the manor-house . . . forms a charming feature of the landscape. It is old and weather-beaten, set in a framework of pines and deciduous trees, with lawns and shrubberies. Look at the beautiful illustration of Manor Hall, near Stroud, with its high gables, tiled roofs, and mul-lioned windows, and compare it with any foreign building of the same size, and you will respect the memories of our English builders.[17]

And then, from the same author two years later, in the opening words to *The Manor Houses of England*:

> England is remarkable for the number and beauty of the old coun-try houses, set amid pleasant scenes, that abound in various parts of our island. Hidden away from the gaze of the multitude in seques-tered villages and obscure hamlets, they are very humble-minded, very retiring. They do not court attention, these English manor-houses, or seek to attract the eye by glaring incongruities or obtru-sive detail. They seem in quest of peace, and love obscurity. . . .
>
> The builders of these houses were animated by that same spirit which moved Sir William Temple, cultured diplomatist, philoso-

pher and garden lover, to write, "The greatest advantages men have by riches are, to give, to build, to plant and make pleasant scenes."[18]

Make pleasant scenes: most people want this, but architecture critics and historians are still reluctant to admit it. Even recent attempts to revive interest in neo-Tudor architecture, mainly the interwar suburban variety of it that is seen everywhere in Britain, have more or less focused on the culture and associations of its style and not much on its actual appearance beyond simple descriptions, while drawing attention to the occasional delightful and unusual feature. Generally these houses have been presented in the form of a kind of challenge to the architectural establishment rather than as a pillar of it, but this is not new.[19] In fact, in his introduction to Batsford's splendid illustrated volume of 1911, *The Domestic Architecture of England During the Tudor Period*, Arthur Stratton wrote:

The Houses described and illustrated in this book will be found to represent the finest examples of the national type of domestic architecture peculiar to England in which there is as yet little attempt to construct a symmetrical facade: the direct methods of planning and simple form of expression which characterize them cannot fail to be rich in suggestion for the present day architect.[20]

FIGURE 2.2
Authentic neo-Tudor houses are now going up everywhere, but almost no one is talking about them. This one in Broadstairs, Kent, dates from around 2000. Courtesy of Keith Diplock.

Indeed, many low-key buildings did emerge from them—a string of Tudor branches of Lloyds Bank, for example, by T. Millwood Wilson, Horace Field's most prolific successor there, but you would not know it if you relied on books on architectural history. It is interesting that when the mainly conservation architects Freeland Rees Roberts completed a large and imaginative neo-Tudor building on the banks of the River Cam, in Cambridge, for Trinity Hall in 1998, no one seems to have had very much to say about it. A modernist building on the same prominent site would surely have generated major articles in all the professional press. In fact neo-Tudor houses now go up all over the place, but no critic says a word. There is still no normal debate about Tudor-style architecture: it is all "fake," apparently.

The concept of "fake" is, of course, the most lasting legacy of Augustus Pugin, as he set about inventing the idea that style was a moral issue and should be addressed *ex cathedra* with absolute rights and wrongs. His most famous book—his *Contrasts* of 1836 and 1841—established in addition the idea that a building can be a fake if its parts are applied to suggest something other than what they actually are. Of churches he says:

> *Unless the ancient arrangement be restored*, and the *true principles carried out*, all mouldings, pinnacles, tracery, and details, be they ever so well executed, are a mere disguise.[21]

"Let then the Beautiful and the True be our watchword" are the stirring words with which he commences the final sentence of *The True Principles* (1841), in effect an instruction book for architects. It is extraordinary how persistent this argument has been; even the arrival of parametric architecture, where everything is "fake" in the Puginian sense, does not seem to have dislodged it much, and even though many modern building materials are no less "fake" than, say, eighteenth-century Coade Stone or nineteenth-century Pulhamite. Not for nothing did David Watkin title the first chapter of his book *Morality and Architecture* simply "Pugin," the first name in a series of architects and writers who, according to the author, diverted architecture away from being about what a building looks like and directed it instead toward what it is made of; as Watkin says, all buildings are artifacts and therefore inherently "fake" anyhow.

FIGURE 2.3
The Jerwood Library at Trinity Hall, Cambridge, completed by Freeland Rees Roberts
Architects in 1998, and ignored by critics. Courtesy of Keith Diplock.

In fact the way in which Pugin's ideas were adopted says a great
deal about the manipulation by the words people of the ideas of the
visual people. My own experience is that for architects, design comes
first, and everything else—from their own descriptions of what they are
trying to do, to their politics, their clothes, and their social con-
science—is simply an attempt at reconciling all those things with their
primary purpose in life. In Pugin's case—and I have been thinking
about this for well over thirty years—it seems to me that he was trying
to drag architecture out of one of its most disappointing and frustrating
periods through the quality of design, and his packaging of the Gothic
Revival as "moral" was part of his attempt at steering his design idea
through to the people who would adopt it and pay for it. This was their
language, and he had to speak it in order to communicate with them.

That does not mean that he did not believe it himself; it simply
means that any talk of "morality" was secondary to his design idea of

clarity, logic, coherence, relevance, and all the other things that he knew were missing from late-Georgian architecture. But as we know, the words people are the dominant ones in culture, and the introduction of the concept of the "fake" marks the start of the early-nineteenth-century onslaught by critics on revivalist styles of architecture that they did not approve of, the first of a number of campaigns that were not only aggressive and rude but also decisively influential, especially since they could now benefit from the new mass media of cheap printing. Pugin himself set a new standard: if the famous plates of *Contrasts* merely made fun of architects great and small, his book *An Apology* contains a great deal of personal or almost-personal abuse, aimed in particular at Charles Cockerell, whose Royal Academy lectures are described as "a perfect disgrace," and whose new University Library at Cambridge was a "monstrous erection of mongrel Italian."[22] The works of the lesser-known John Shaw at Pugin's own school, Christ's Hospital in the City of London, were "sad failures"; and as for John Soane's extensions to the Bank of England, they were "the most costly masses of absurdities that have ever been erected"; Bartholomew had a go at Soane, too.[23] No doubt one can find rude remarks about unfashionable or perhaps overfashionable styles of architecture from any point in history before this—some very funny things were said by those who resented the takeover of English state and aristocratic architecture by untalented neo-Palladians from the hands of brilliant baroque designers at the beginning of the eighteenth century—but it is fair to say that like much else in Anglo-Saxon culture, the tendency to take up a hectoring, bullying approach on the matter of style, of all things, is an invention of the first half of the nineteenth century.[24]

LOOKING AT HOUSES THE WAY NOVELISTS DO

Novelists are not like this; they are not in the business of classifying their houses into types along the lines traditionally preferred by architectural critics, and with the exception of the writers of fairy tales they do not generally establish moral wrongs in architecture which need to be attacked. What they are sometimes aiming for is the mood of the thing, which can express itself through a number of narrative events—some happy, some tragic, and not necessarily related to each other, conveyed by a few key visual elements. There are quite different ways of doing this. In Charles Dickens's novels, a house often crudely represents a mood—a pleasant person generally lives in a pleasant house; on the other hand, the houses of Honoré de Balzac are realistically depicted so as to make precise points about their inhabitants and their movements within: the house of Eugénie Grandet in Saumur, for example, from the novel of the same name (1833), is so accurately represented that it would be perfectly possible to draw it up from the description on the page at a quarter inch to the foot. Here is a lesson in understanding architecture that quite a few of our losers—the sentimental ones, the ones with the unfashionable romantic styles—are more aware of than our leading architectural critics. Put at its most simple, a dining room may take on a tragic air because of an event that happens there; the feeling remains in the room, perhaps for a generation, exactly as if it was an architectural element rather than an event. When handled deftly by a writer, a personalized, literary description—that is, a parallel kind of architectural critique of a building—can elicit a much deeper and more informed response from the onlooker than conventional architectural judgment can manage.

Alan Hollinghurst's recent novel *The Stranger's Child* provides a strong demonstration of this. There are two principal houses in this novel, and each represents one of the major characters: one is suburban and the other aristocratic, a contrast much liked in English literature and familiar to many, especially through Evelyn Waugh's *Brideshead Revisited*. Hollinghurst's story opens in 1913, and the first of his houses is "Two Acres," the comfortable new home of George Dawe in Stanmore, in the then still largely rural county of Middlesex, now absorbed into north and west London. It so happens that this house, which gives its name to the first section of the book, is located both geographically and chronologically close to Horace Field's beautiful but now devastated branch of Lloyds Bank in Wealdstone, although it is hard to imagine that Hollinghurst was aware of that. Perhaps, actually, Field was the architect of the fictional "Two Acres" as well, for there was a house designed by him at 37 Gordon Avenue in Stanmore that suits the description, but we cannot check it out because—like several of Field's best houses—it has been demolished, and in this case partly replaced, by nice if paradoxical coincidence, by a road called Greenacres Drive.

The story begins with the visit of George's aristocratic university friend and poet Cecil Valance to Stanmore, and preparations are made in the different areas of the house to receive him. What is striking is that the building is not presented to start with as an overall form with a specific description: different areas of it receive detailed treatment, and readers are left to assemble them in their own mind. The narrative starts outside in the garden, just as the lamps are being lit inside; it then touches on the interior of the sitting room, and moves up to the spare bedroom where Valance's suitcase is being unpacked by a young servant. It moves briefly into George's brother's bedroom, into the hall, and then into the dining room. The action then returns to the sitting room and in fact emphasizes the open windows onto the garden, a device that recalls to the reader the opening pages of the book. It is only after the story is under way that George refers to the house as having "a way of 'resolving itself into nooks'"; elsewhere the house is referred to as being arts and crafts in style, and it has a folksy, slightly comic street number: 2A.[25]

What is remarkable about this episodic mode of presenting a house is how different it is from the way it would be if it were an example given in an architectural textbook, or how we would teach students to write about a building. There is no overall description of form or style. There is no "concept." There is not even necessarily any stylistic consistency. Certain specific areas become associated with the feelings and expressions of the people discovered within them. The furniture is highly likely to be as important as the architecture of the rooms. It would be possible to interpret Hollinghurst's description of "Two Acres" as a conventional piece of phenomenology, and yet this would be in my view inadequate. Phenomenology is a winners' perspective: it attributes meaning to the spaces by virtue of the associations they arouse. Yet it is possible to put this familiar approach precisely into reverse, and say that the elements of the house are here created by the associations that frame it. "Two Acres" is presented as the setting for a pair of contrasting homosexual situations: one in which two attractive university under-graduates, who in later sections of the story both turn out to be straight, have the kind of sex one associates with Edwardian aesthetes, with much fresh air, swimming, and poetry; the other in which a plain and straight young man, George's lonely and inadequate brother, much given to masturbation, is pursued ardently but hopelessly by an older and richer man until he meets a sad end. There is no separation between the house and these situations: they are as inseparable as a Balzac *roué* is from his Paris *hôtel*. The architecture therefore is sentimental, romantic, and somewhat arch—its whole purpose is to frame the scene. When Hollinghurst talks about lamps, a glow, "a small round table," "a gloomy little room by the front door," "a nice old Sheraton cabinet," he is urging us by degrees to have a sense of what a building can provide as a backdrop for personal relationships.[26]These are warm, comforting materials and details, and the general sense of them is more valuable than an exact delineation. Loudon was, I think, going in this direction when he describes toward the end of his *Encyclopaedia* how a few but important accumulated possessions—a marriage chest, for example—start to give even a small house narrative value.[27]

Hollinghurst's treatment of "Two Acres" comes naturally to anyone who reads a novel, just as it was natural for anyone who specialized in painting interior genre scenes to follow similar rules, but for some reason architecture critics who have set their minds against sentimentality cannot understand it. It is a familiar tool for novelists, and one sees it all the time; it was thought by some reviewers that *The Stranger's Child* owes something to E. M. Forster's authentically Edwardian *Howards End*, in which a much older house is presented as a metaphor for a family rooted in English soil, a quality lost by the house-renting, town-dwelling modern generation. Interestingly, Elizabeth Bowen set a key scene in her novel *Eva Trout* (1969) in a house called "Cathay" of similar age and style to "Two Acres" but at North Foreland, the bleak easternmost point of Thanet in Kent, ten minutes' walk from my own home. This one was built "around 1908," was modernized between the wars and bomb-scarred, and exactly as with Hollinghurst it is presented in the form of fragments; in fact the style of the house is revealed only in very small ones: "deep ornamental eaves . . . leaded windows . . . oak just too black to be old . . . a *manoir*-style dining-room suite . . . the bay window at the seaward end of the drawing-room contained a loveseat—originally, a gilded one."[28] Everything that is important about the building, including its detachment from security and normality, everything that anyone needs to recognize in order to understand the significance of the house to the story, is conveyed by a few words; and everything else about the building that is important to the plot is revealed by the few activities that Eva herself does in there. *Romantic Moderns*, Alexandra Harris's survey of the English aesthetic fashions of the early twentieth century, dwells on the work of Bowen, seeing her as the novelist whose buildings and their contents are alive, or breathing, staring or dying.[29] If only architectural critics could be as sensitive and sympathetic to the hidden joys of quiet architecture as Harris, who is an art historian.

I suspect that the unrecognized architects who designed houses like "Two Acres" would have seen their houses pretty much the way Hollinghurst depicts his at the start of his novel: episodically, sentimentally, romantically, allusively. We can assume that in around 1890, if that is when his house was built, they were not, knowingly, phenomenologists themselves. Unlike Hollinghurst, they would not have known that the arts and crafts style was one that now would have an

FIGURE 2.4
One of several interwar houses at North Foreland in Kent that closely match the novelist Elizabeth Bowen's imaginary "Cathay." Courtesy of Keith Diplock.

aura of decadence about it. Unlike Hollinghurst, they were not seeing into a future when "Two Acres" is mutilated and on the verge of demolition, its secrets burnt in an uncaring bonfire by shabby, ugly people in what remains of the garden. These Edwardian architects had a sense of how they wanted the various parts of the building to work and feel. They were a bit like the high-art architect's most feared client, the one who wants a kitchen like the one they saw at a friend's house, but also a dining room in the different style they saw on a television makeover show. Their view of architecture was not that of the artist-designer who defines a form, a theory, a concept, before starting work on details. In Michael Cunningham's devastating short novel *By Nightfall* the art dealer protagonist arrives at the house of a client when he is himself in a state of emotional turmoil and, not surprisingly, he takes in the grand mansion as if it were a jumbled collection of fragments of building: it seems like an "enormous rambling house," the interiors of which are a collection of unrelated set pieces: Bach, French doors, Jean-Michel Frank, Giacometti, Art Deco, Dogon.[30] Thus one feels both the decadence of the client's taste and the confusion of the protagonist's mind; one knows enough about what the house is like without any overall presentation in words.

All of this would have been understood by architects of the era of "Two Acres" and "Cathay," and it is easy to find evidence of that through popular books on domestic architecture: in fact most contemporary publications on the subject illustrated them in precisely that way. Books like W. Shaw Sparrow's *Flats, Urban Houses and Cottage Homes* (1907) provide images and brief descriptions of many new suburban houses built in the fertile period between 1890 and 1914, generally organized by size or cost so that a prospective client could see what their budget would afford. Interior and detailed images are chosen not so much to demonstrate an architectural "concept" as a sentimental one, and to give a characterful picture of a distinct space. Sometimes an architect has provided a hand-drawn perspective in the form of a vignette which could easily, in retrospect, be a scene from Hollinghurst or Bowen.

A tiny number of houses in these books are by architects whose names have survived to posterity, and it is generally obvious from their contributions why they have been remembered. But as far as the great

narrative of architectural history is concerned, the rest of these architects are failures, because there is no conventional and accepted architectural narrative about them. It was of their work (and possibly of his
own) that the architect and critic Harry Goodhart-Rendel was speaking when he wrote that the "quiet good taste of the tired Edwardian
smells badly of decay."[31] And yet it is surely obvious by now that these
people with the quiet good taste had a great deal of impact on visual
experience and daily life, with the endless suburban houses that they
built, and much to say about what their designers intended to go on in
them. If the architect of "Two Acres" was a good one, he might well
have been able to define an appealing overall mood or a style in his
designs, and this will have brought him clients; but we all know that
designers with this glib felicity get short shrift from the critics, and we
hardly know the names of any of them today outside the occasional
detailed study in an academic journal. Picturesque, romantic, sentimental and professional *successful* architects like Charles Mallows, who
drew and built gorgeous houses before the First World War, live in a
parallel universe as far as most architecture critics and historians are
concerned.

I was reminded of Hollingurst's story—and in particular the phrase
"resolving itself into nooks"—when I read *Edwardian Country Life*,
Helena Gerrish's study of the gardener and architectural writer H.
Avray Tipping. Tipping, who graduated from Oxford with Oscar
Wilde, was a central figure in the Edwardian aesthetic establishment;
he was a friend of Edwin Lutyens and of the interior designer and
landscape architect Harold Peto; as a writer for *Country Life* magazine,
which championed Lutyens and Gertrude Jekyll, his taste in house and
garden design was influential. He was to a minor extent an architect
himself, and he collaborated in the design of his own houses—he was
an incessant builder—with a young professional, Eric Carwardine
Francis. He maintained close, lifelong friendships with an architect
called George Herbert Kitchin and with Christopher Hussey, his successor as architectural writer at *Country Life*, but he never married; in
fact he inexplicably left nearly all his substantial estate—he was, like
Peto, the son of a prosperous railway builder—to his 31-year-old gardener, Walter Ernest Wood, who had become a kind of awkward
adopted son to him.[32] This in interwar Britain, where class distinctions

would normally have rendered such things unthinkable. The last house that Francis helped Tipping build for himself was called High Glanau Manor, near Monmouth in the far southeast of Wales. Although it was not designed until the mid-1920s, it is an arts and crafts house that very much "resolves itself into nooks." The interior is, mostly, Jacobean in style, with deep exposed timber joists and decorative plaster ceilings. It is here that Tipping sat alone in his old age, day after day, with the occasional visit from the gardener for company. Who knows what joy the sound of the approaching footsteps of that awkward young man used to bring here. Or terror, perhaps. This house and its story seem to me to conjure up a combination of the ordinary and the devastating.

What interests me about both Hollinghurst's imagined arts and crafts house and Tipping's real one is that the period in which they emerged is exactly that in which critical commentary on some of our most sensitive architecture was abandoned, on both sides of the Atlantic, just as it had been abandoned under the onslaught of the Gothic Revival almost a hundred years before. Writers about the early twentieth century are already looking for novelty rather than sentiment. That adds to the sense of the failure of these places—they are for us, looking back, a dying breed; lingering over the black-and-white photographs in books like Shaw Sparrow's adds to what Ruskin would have called their "twilight melancholy," their gentle fading on their way out; they are buildings about which there is no discourse in architectural criticism, and so they are failures. Architectural history is not about them. And yet so many of them were beautifully composed, detailed and built, and became filled with powerful memories for many people.

NOT INTERESTING

Nowadays, the literary supplement of a broadsheet newspaper will contain reviews of many books which are perfectly decent but no more than second- or third-rate; indeed, a third-rate biography will generate perhaps 10, 20, 30 times the amount of critical coverage that a first-rate book on architectural history will ever receive, and could sell 100 times more copies.[33] So architectural history is "not interesting," evidently, and I would claim that this is because of the way in which it is talked about. Compare this situation with what happens in the other arts, even the minority ones. The poetry program put out by the BBC's Radio 4, its principal speech station, will mainly consist of second-rate or amateur verse, some very sentimental, and yet judging by its popularity it is enjoyable for those who listen. The only place where second-rate or unfashionable architecture is likely to get an airing is in the weekly journals of the architectural profession, close to the time of its completion; and even then it is only in exceptional circumstances that a building in a historical style, or a variation of it, will attract any attention. The British *Architects' Journal* of the 1920s and 1930s contains hundreds of buildings that only scholars in limited fields will ever look at again. And then these disappointing, derivative failure-buildings vanish, at any rate from everything but the academic and the nostalgic press, and in the case of houses they linger on only in the many glossy magazines that deal with decorating and interior design. And they survive there because the language of those magazines is the language of the novelist, of the sentimentalist, of the stylist—it is about rooms, feelings, vignettes; about comfort, coziness, retiral, leisure. It is not the attack language of the architecture critic.

This is not to say that there is no prominent or significant writing and publishing on non-modernist styles of architecture in either Britain or America. Of this there is plenty. Since the 1980s there have been many books on neoclassical architecture, at any rate. In both Britain and the United States there have been several high-profile studies of neoclassicists that have entered the canon: in the United States the process was perhaps launched by the first of several publications on Robert A. M. Stern, in 1981; the heavy, glossy monograph on the work of John Russell Pope in 1991 seems to mark a watershed, and certainly after the appearance of *Allen Greenberg* in 1997 it has been easy to find good-quality, well-illustrated writing, just as the spreading fame of projects such as Seaside, and the progress of the New Urbanism movement in general, must have contributed to the rise of architectural practices which specialize in neoclassical architecture. Glossy monographs are generally funded by their subjects, after all. Sometimes these publications have a triumphalist air to them, reacting consciously and proudly to what Vincent Scully in 1994 called "the tight hold (like that of the Marine Corps or the Catholic Church) which the architectural profession exerts on anyone who has ever belonged to it."[34] At any rate, they are not about retiral or retreat, or any of the important elements I have emphasized in the quiet architecture of the early twentieth century.

The triumphalist tendency is particularly evident in comparable British books, such as David Watkin's *Radical Classicism: The Architecture of Quinlan Terry*, or in the outspoken criticisms of modernist architecture by revivalists such as Robert Adam, because British writers have been reacting to such narrow conventions in architectural criticism. Over here it is still broadly Puginite and Pevsnerite, to which Peter Davey, during the long period in which he was editor of the dominant *Architectural Review*—nearly a quarter of a century, from 1982 to 2005—added a moral commitment toward sustainability and public service. So such pro-traditionalist writing as there has been seems to have come as a reaction to the limitations of architectural criticism in general, rather than anything more positive or realistic; antimodernist writers clearly enjoy attacking the shibboleths of liberal culture, each side no doubt intentionally provoking their target into new heights of incivility.

Thus my argument is that mainstream architectural criticism has failed to address attempts to work with what look like traditional types of building or variations on them—including, for example, versions of earlier incarnations of modernist or eclectic architecture—and this has left a large hole in architectural debate. Such opposing voices as there are seem trapped within the same game, reacting to a culture of attack rather than promoting what is good. As a result, architectural criticism is much the weaker, and further detached from the experience of everyday life, especially where the principal themes of a building are to do with retreat and retrenchment. In Britain, at least, there has been a serious attempt to rewrite a conventional narrative that was dominated by the view that architecture was involved in an endless march toward progress and technological proficiency: prominent among the contributors to this have been Gavin Stamp, Alan Powers, and Kenneth Powell, all of whom have championed some lesser-known practitioners who worked in variants of historical styles. Powers's *Britain*, an outline of twentieth-century architecture in the country, downplays, for example, the roles of the well-known Brutalist and modernist controversialists, while placing an unprecedented degree of emphasis on the work of small, quiet practices such as that of Hubert Tayler and David Green, which up to that point was almost certainly unknown to all but a handful of the book's many professional, academic, and student readers.

The case of Raymond Erith, the mid-twentieth-century neoclassical architect who saw himself beginning where Soane left off, and did achieve critical recognition and was widely published, illustrates the problem that the traditional good-versus-bad dichotomy in architectural criticism poses: it seems impossible to place him in any conventional architectural narrative, despite the public prominence of the buildings he designed. According to Powell, the only modernist master Erith had any time for was Mies van der Rohe, since he saw himself as a structural purist who laid as much emphasis on both the structural expression and the constructional composition of a building as did Mies himself.[35] And yet what is so striking about Erith's work is that it has a wistful, indefinable quality, in part because his unfamiliar composition of Soanean and Regency-era detailing is unfamiliar, rather as if one had come across it in a dream. In his internal courtyard to 10 Downing Street, a project no older than myself, a colonnade of Corinthian columns seems to have sunk into the ground, as if the modern house above were merely some kind of perfunctory residence that might have gone up over a half-buried temple 300 years ago—a clever and funny idea, beautifully designed and executed. Erith's Provost's Lodgings at Queen's College, Oxford (1958–1960), presents an almost blank façade to the street: a Regency ivory tower, perhaps. His detailing here and elsewhere was often exquisite. Powell observed that although Erith, as a Royal Academician and architect to the government and the gentry, was a member of the establishment, it was not the architectural establishment he had joined but the political and social one, the two being completely at odds with one another when Erith was at his most creative and productive.[36] Mainstream architectural criticism has simply never known what to do with Erith's work, because it was "pastiche," or "fake." David Watkin maintains that the use of the term "pastiche" to describe the recent deployment of a historical or traditional style is necessarily derogatory, because it assumes that historical traditions are not capable of being living ones.

SHRINKING, HOPING, FADING

Erith was also an unassuming person, and perhaps he had no special
interest in or talent for self-publicity. It was his shrinking from self-pro-
motion that caused Vasari to label Andrea del Sarto as an artist who
failed to fulfill his potential in the early sixteenth century, and it still
makes a difference today. To give a recent example, Mark Lamster has
recently written in the *Architectural Review* of Tod Williams and Billy
Tsien that

> Superstardom hasn't happened for them, and perhaps by design.
> They seem content to run their practice as an atelier . . . the two
> tend to let their work speak for itself, and it speaks with a quiet
> seriousness of purpose that is easily and sadly overlooked.[37]

He went on to say that at a recent press conference for their newly
completed Barnes Foundation collection in Philadelphia, a large and
prestigious project that they must have spent years thinking about and
working through, they had nothing to say but to express their thanks to
their client—in marked contrast to those well-known architects with
international reputations (Lamster suggested Daniel Libeskind and
Rem Koolhaas) who would have exploited the occasion to give a philo-
sophical, self-publicizing address. As Hugh Casson put it in 1953, "All
professional people . . . depend very largely on bluff, whether they are
dentists, veterinary surgeons, or architects."[38]

It is not impossible that physical retreat, up a hillside or to an isolated village, perhaps allied with disgust at modern methods of self-
promotion, has prevented talented architects from achieving
recognition, and then in turn the jobs that would have made them
more obviously a success: Peter Blundell Jones says that in his opinion
this is true of David Lea, whose best-known work, the residential
buildings at the Royal Agricultural College at Cirencester in Gloucestershire, are, interestingly, designed in a modern neo-Tudor vernacular; Lea has no website (at any rate, not one that is findable by
Googling) and is located far from any architectural community, at an
address which, being in Welsh, is unpronounceable to most English
speakers, located outside the small town of Penrhyndeudraeth and just

within the edges of the Snowdonia National Park.[39] Proclaiming to audiences and putting out press releases; pressing the buttons of well-known critics; going on about the utter newness of everything; the authenticity of something (the plan, the materials, whatever); the talking in political, moral and social terms, the talking, the talking—are these really what make a building worth a conversation? And, more importantly, is this the way good design is recognized and nurtured?

It seems to me, then, in conclusion, that some architecture is unfairly treated because it has been the victim of noisy and aggressive attacks from people who have succeeded in getting their voices heard, and because it has not found a language among architecture critics to describe it. The result is that large areas of architecture which are perfectly decent, if not excellent, are in many ways ignored or underrated. It is possible to appreciate buildings beyond the confines of the language of conventional architectural criticism, for example by talking about the hopes, failed or otherwise, that buildings express; their details; the lives and the people in them; even what they are not. It is not necessary that all parts of a building should be coherent, or demonstrate a "concept": a building can be at war with itself, something we will look at later. Every now and then an architect speaks with a sudden candor that tells us a great deal. Herbert Tayler, of Tayler and Green, British architects whose postwar public housing in Norfolk was designed in a Scandinavian "New Empiricist" style and who of course condemned "sentimentality," as every architect feels they have to, told Elain Harwood in 1996:

> We realised that having broken away from the international modern stuff, functional style if you like, that people lacked decoration and enjoyment in the look of the houses and so we introduced sorts of colours, different colours for each house, brick patterns, dates. The date of the terrace in the raised brickwork and this was an immediate success. Everybody liked it, people do like decoration.[40]

In other words, the details of the design of the terrace were sentimental, but well done and in good taste nevertheless. He spoke not like an architect but as if he were an ordinary person who has found something he likes in the street.

BULLIES AND SISSIES

FASCISTS, COMMUNISTS, AND MARGARET THATCHER

Right at the start of the introduction we saw Pugin shouting down a scheme by Basevi for new buildings at Balliol College, Oxford, and in chapter 2 he was rubbishing other architects. In the twentieth century violent attacks became the normal way of talking about buildings. Early-century manifestos by polemicists—Loos, Le Corbusier, Gropius—provide rich examples, and the fact that modernist architectural historians, unlike everybody else, generally like to write in terms of revolutions and breakthroughs, and post-rationalized intellectual debates, rather than slow developments, has reinforced and established them. Until recent times student crits were aggressive events where guest critics vied with tutors to make the cleverest, nastiest remarks they could; presumably this stopped when boys began to cry as well as girls, and students were invited, in the public universities at any rate, to fill out feedback forms on the quality of the response they were receiving from their teachers. One event that sticks in my mind came when a tutor at the The Bartlett School of Architecture encouraged us during the course of a fifth-year crit to comment on a fellow student's scheme. We were designing a city airport for London. "Why is there such a contrast between the width of the circulation areas in the departure hall, and the narrowness of the route from the departure hall to the boarding gate?" I asked. This was met with silence from the crittee. When it was my turn to put my work up on the wall, that same student rubbished it time and time again, in waves of fury. He is now the named partner of one of the best-known architectural practices in the world, so there is little doubt which of us came out the loser.

Certain aspects of design always attracted a vicious response from any critic who happened to be looking at it. At Cambridge we had two students who insisted on designing in a neo-Georgian style. They never got any kind of reasonable response from their tutors; this in a department with a fabulous library collection of books on neoclassical architecture a few seconds' walk from the studio. No tutor ever said to them: "Go and look at . . .". Not once, as I recall. And of course the more the tutors attacked them, the more defensive they grew about their ideas, so that they became in effect unteachable and untaught. I designed a scheme in my first term—October 1979—in what I hoped would be a Ralph Erskine kind of style—I loved Clare Hall, the post-graduate college on the other side of the River Cam—and I was given a personal lecture by a visiting critic about the evils of Margaret Thatcher, recently elected. The pretext for this appeared to be that my building was not abstract, white, and rectangular (as opposed to abstract, white, and a funny shape, the late-modernist alternative). I think the rationale was as follows: Thatcher, controversially among liberals, opposed the building of public housing, and public housing was largely uniform in style, so a person who designed housing in a more colorful way was therefore some kind of libertarian nut-job. Looking back, I can see that I was irritating as a student. I used to tell people that I preferred the Cambridge University's elevated faculties building designed by Casson, Conder and Partners off Sidgwick Avenue to James Stirling's neigh-boring and famous History Faculty—then in a process of accelerated decay, with tiles flying off and nasty chemical reactions going on around the windows—and when he heard this, my director of studies told me that this was "proof that I wasn't fit to be an architect." If you make the argument in favor of Casson Conder now—and I have heard fashionable critics doing it—you are praised for your sensitivity to English Scandinavianism. There is no particular reason why teachers should be soft on students who need discipline—who sometimes need a boot up the backside to learn to look, to analyze, to research, to think—but on the other hand, the sliding into narrow political polemic, unrelated to anything visual, and the closing down of areas of discus-sion, is unlikely to do much good either.

The business about Margaret Thatcher is a significant one, because it is typical of the mid- to late-twentieth-century process of automatically associating a style with a political movement: neoclassical = Speer, as it were. The fact that architectural debate is certainly political does not justify a cheap and lazy association of a style or an attempt at it with a complete and unrelated political attitude.[1] If you know that an individual votes for a certain party, you still know very little about that person, and virtually nothing at all about their creative instincts; as I have said before, in my experience everything about an architect, from their clothes to their politics and their religion, is derived first and foremost from their architecture.

Looking back through old journals, it appears that there was one key moment when the architectural press seems to have made a concerted effort to establish a link between architecture and politics, and used it effectively to change the way in which buildings were talked about. This came when Erich Mendelsohn won with Serge Chermayeff the competition to design an entertainments pavilion at Bexhill-on-Sea, in Sussex on the south coast of England, in 1934. By reprinting some letters on the competition from members of the British Union of Fascists that had previously appeared in small-circulation local and political newspapers, the *Architects' Journal*, the weekly paper then widely read by British architects, conjured up an artificial storm for its own quite different readership. Earlier in the year it had published letters by, and addressing comments from, a prominent British fascist, and the Bexhill business gave its writers an opportunity to air their politics again.

The editor of the *Architects' Journal* was the proprietor's son, Hubert de Cronin Hastings, who himself took a political stance on architecture, but since 1934 his small team had been joined by J. M. Richards, a neighbor and friend of Mendelsohn, a pro-modernist and a Communist sympathizer.[2] At the time of the Bexhill competition, the pages of the *Journal* were full of neo-Georgian town halls and even the occasional rustic cottage—in this respect it was somewhat old-fashioned when compared to its drier professional rival, the *Architect & Building News*. This had already gone modernist; the assistant editor was Richards's friend John Summerson, with whom the former saw himself in friendly rivalry. It seems likely that Richards, who soon had

FIGURE 3.1
The competition-winning De La Warr Pavilion by Erich Mendelsohn
and Serge Chermayeff at Bexhill-on-Sea, Sussex (1934): the pretext for
the *Architects' Journal*'s move to modernism. Courtesy of the author.

a "growing role" at the magazine, managed the Bexhill story, and perhaps it was he who had recently found the Bexhill Pavilion "virile"—a
compliment, of course—by comparison to the latest batch of municipal
Georgiana in the journal's unsigned Notes and Topics column.[3]

Mendelsohn's design was published in February 1934, when there
would have been considerable interest among British architects in the
fate of their profession under fascism; but the way in which the *Architects' Journal* managed to prolong the subject of the pavilion in its cor-
respondence columns over the period that followed hints at a calculated
intention of softening up its readership for the magazine's wholesale
conversion to modern architecture. The fascist, or at any rate xenopho-
bic, reaction to Mendelsohn provided the editors with an effective
Aunt Sally. In January 1935 it published, for example, a letter from a
Keith Aitken of Cardiff, who, we read, observed:

> The tragedy of the Jew appears to be his unfailing ability to arouse
> antagonism wherever he goes . . . we must be on our guard against
> too readily drinking in Jewish-Communist doctrine, even when it
> is disguised in the most seductive of concrete and glass clothes.[4]

As the *Architects' Journal* recognized, the antagonism to Mendelsohn was not really based on the foreignness of his architecture. All the published runner-up schemes for Bexhill were provincial, fairground versions of the style that Mendelsohn himself had invented, including a second-placed scheme by the fascist sympathizer Marshall Sisson with James Burford; it seems hardly surprising that he could do it better than his competitors. The real challenge to Mendelsohn was his foreignness, if not his Jewishness. This episode enabled the magazine to portray the enemies of international modernism as simultaneously the enemies of liberty and progress, or even as xenophobes and anti-Semites; there were plenty of liberal correspondents to agree with the editorial line. By 1935 there were enough modernist projects around for Richards and Hastings to publish at least one every week, and Richards departed to continue his work at the monthly *Architectural Review*, the *Architects' Journal*'s sister magazine. In 1951 he became a long-serving member of the influential Royal Final Arts Commission, the body that then bestowed *de haut en bas* backing to major or controversial architectural projects, a position from which he was able to continue his campaign for modernism until a volte-face that seems to have occurred by 1972.[5]

A sad footnote to the Bexhill affair is that Richards soon joined the long list of people who had taken a dislike to Mendelsohn as a person. By the time he visited the recently completed De La Warr Pavilion, named for the national politician and benefactor who was also the local mayor, he had decided that Mendelsohn was only "friendly to those he thought could be useful to him."[6] Richards does not mention the *Architects' Journal*'s exploitation to political ends of the Bexhill competition in his memoirs, and that leads me to think that he felt duped. This story from 1934 to 1935 marks the point from which high-art architecture once more became distinct from the great body of buildings; furthermore, it also sees the start of the process by which interior design magazines set off on an entirely independent path, to the extent that they have now become happily and ludicrously ignored by architecture critics the world over.

SHOW TRIALS

Hugh Casson, naively mentioned earlier by my 18-year-old self, was seen at that time in the late 1970s as a figure of particular ridicule. His popular image was derived from his success as Director of Architecture at the Festival of Britain, the high-water mark of the Scandinavianists—that is, the British architects who designed in the style, sometimes then called "Contemporary," that was adapted from the Swedish and Danish architecture of the 1940s as it appeared in the otherwise thin *Architectural Review* of the period, or as they saw it on subsequent pilgrimages to Stockholm, Gothenburg, Copenhagen, and Århus.[7] It was Casson who for a while thereafter enjoyed the privilege of recommending architects for prestigious public commissions. He was a friend and consultant to the royal family; he was an establishment figure, as President of the Royal Academy of Arts, as well as being, like Richards, a long-serving member (1960–1983) of the Royal Fine Arts Commission; and his name was associated with schemes that were actually mainly designed or executed by other people, for example his partner Neville Conder, or, to his greater disadvantage, with clumsy buildings by other architects who had at some stage received advice from him: my local town hall in Margate, actually by the otherwise unknown Fewster & Partners, is one of these.[8] No doubt his "ability to charm people by conversational wit," as a biographer puts it, annoyed the angry young men even more.[9] I once came across Casson in the late 1980s: a tiny figure, sitting on a London bus, writing some notes on a pad shortly after an attack by Charles, Prince of Wales, on modern architecture in the form of his television program "A Vision of Britain" which, among other things, had compared some major modernist buildings in London to a nuclear bunker and an academy for secret policemen, the classicist's response to the still aggressive face of modernist criticism. Sitting beside my hero on the longitudinal seats by the bottom of the stairs in an old Routemaster bus, and squinting hard, I cautiously cast a glance across at his notepad. "The prince is right in what he is saying, but wrong in the way he says it," wrote Sir Hugh in his neat italic script. I was appalled that so great a man, who had created through the Festival and its many children a cheerful, bright, optimistic architecture, should be reduced to having to use his powers of diplomacy to respond to so vulgar and silly an attack at all. And what this episode also impressed on me was that being polite, and charming, and conciliatory, as Casson was, simply placed him further in the firing line for a brutal attack, and made it harder for him to respond.

It took about twenty years for attacks on British Scandinavianist architects, from the late 1940s to the late 1960s, to become established to the extent that the modernist, and then the Brutalist-conceptualist, interpretations of architecture became the only ones to appear in narrative accounts of twentieth-century British architecture. Brutalism is considered by some to have been launched with a short, italicized, gnomic comment by Alison Smithson (although attributed in print to Peter Smithson) in the journal *Architectural Design* in December 1953, accompanying a design for a house in Soho:

> *It is our intention in this building to have the structure exposed entirely, without internal finishes wherever practicable. The Contractor should aim at a high standard of basic construction, as in a small warehouse.*[10]

This sounds intimidating, almost violent, for the design of a private house, and it suited the aggressive polemical language of the Smithsons, who elsewhere talked of imposing the grit and masculinity they associated with northern working-class housing onto the delicate inhabitants of the south, for no good (or explained) reason. This sort of thing is locker-room intimidation, really; cock-flashing, threatening, as it was no doubt intended to be; and it had an inspiring effect on the young architects who simply found the Scandinavianist architecture of the period dull. That in itself this was not surprising, for the buildings were indeed often dull, and had changed little between the end of the war and the early 1950s; even those with a Scandinavianist disposition would find the aggressive work of upcoming architects such as James Stirling and James Gowan exciting.[11] But what is extraordinary is the way in which this absurd minority view, this championing of rawness and grit, with no logic, no evidence, or anything realistic at all behind it to support it, and, most of all, no relationship to how life is actually lived and experienced, managed to root itself into the canons of architectural history produced over the following decades to such an extent that the Scandinavianists fell eventually beneath the stylistic and intellectual radar for most critics. If they were mentioned at all, it was with vehement derision. Kenneth Frampton wrote a chapter on this period in postwar British architecture in his *Modern Architecture*, still widely read by students; it dismisses the Contemporary style as "popular" before hurrying on to what really interests him. There is nothing here at all on the romantic nature of its arrival as the dream style of wartime fighters and little on the imagery that, through the New Towns and prestigious projects such as Alton East, the Brutalist Alton West's less appreciated neighbor, set the tone for some ten years in British public housing, right across the country.[12] Indeed, the book makes no reference whatsoever to any human quality or sensitivity, or romance, or vision, in any building at all. It then alights on an easy target—Basil Spence, a Scandinavianist at first, a romantic and a stylist and, like Casson, an establishment figure, rather than a theorist or teacher. *Modern Architecture* gratuitously throws in a reference to the "absolute banality" of Spence's Coventry cathedral of 1951–1962, by any standards an extraordinarily dismissive remark to make about a complicated and rich project such as this. The most memorable point about the cathedral, the aspect of it that strikes every visitor, is that it was devised as a kind of shrine for the works of artists of one of the richest periods in the British applied arts: Graham Sutherland, Jacob Epstein, John Piper, Patrick Reyntiens, John Hutton, Elisabeth Frink, Ralph Beyer, Geoffrey Clarke, and many others.[13] In this way it forms the closest equivalent to the rich interior of a pre-Reformation church that the Church of England has offered since the First World War. So, first of all, the architecture critic was separating the carcass of Spence's building from what was within it, perhaps because of a horror of getting involved with anything sentimental, in this case embodied by the personal and devotional nature of the objects within. This is surely something that no non-architect visitor would do. It is also inconsistent with critical practice, because it is accepted that earlier high-art interiors, for example of arts and crafts houses, were part of the fundamental concept of the architect who designed them.[14] And then secondly, even the form of Spence's building is disregarded, presumably because neither Spence himself nor any contemporary critic talked about it in conceptual or sculptural terms, or because there is nothing obviously peculiar about it. This too is bizarre, because even a brief look at the zigzag sandstone walls and deep mullioned windows of the cathedral tells an interesting story about how a Scottish architect who was immersed in the traditional architecture of his country, who grew up with the interwar interpretations of it, and who was captivated by Scandinavianism, managed to bring all three to life in a single building in a historic English city completely destroyed by war. In addition, the linking of the ruins of the old building with the new one, the aspect of Spence's design that probably won him the competition, is a significant statement about how people in Britain wanted to reconnect their picturesque tradition with the desperate ruined state of their cities. These are all big stories, I think, that many people can relate to. And yet what interests Frampton instead is, absurdly, the Smithsons' unsuccessful Brutalist entry for the Coventry competition, which he described as "mediated Palladianism," a phrase surely unintelligible to anyone reading it or looking at a representation of the proposal.[15] How did the Smithsons work their magic? Alan Powers is putting it diplomatically when he describes them as "the clever but disruptive children

FIGURE 3.2
St. Michael's Cathedral, Coventry, won in competition by Basil Spence in 1950 and derided by modernist critics for some 30 years afterward. Courtesy of Keith Diplock.

of a Modern Movement that thought it had settled down for a con-
formist middle age, [who] justified their rebellion with a rare innate
sense of architecture and a personal manner in which arrogance was
combined with a vulnerable kind of directness": in everyday language,
what this means is that in Powers's judgment, they were gratuitously
rude, and much of what they said about architecture was self-evident
nonsense.[16] In the words of Jonathan Meades, the British critic who
makes a point of puncturing the literary pretensions of architects and
of seeing buildings the way normal people do, "in the pantheon of
Brutalists they come way, way down."[17] And yet look where they are—
admired by architects and especially architecture students the world
over, the subject of endless books and articles, a tribute to the power of
verbal bullying.

The Brutalist architect Denys Lasdun longed for "a terrible battle
with architecture," by which he meant a battle against civility and con-
formity.[18] In the 1970s Charles Jencks was still fighting it: his book
Modern Movements in Architecture compared Frederick Gibberd's
Roman Catholic cathedral in Liverpool (a loser-building, because it sits
on Edwin Lutyens's crypt, as we have seen) predictably and unflatter-
ingly to Oscar Niemeyer's cathedral at Brasília (roughly the same shape,
but otherwise unrelated); to Marcel Breuer's work in general; and, inexplicably, to Le Corbusier's Unité d'Habitation, comparisons which are
illogical and unhelpful. Like Frampton he deployed the phrase "people's
detailing"—here characterized by "pitched roofs, bricky materials, ticky-
tacky, cute lattice work, little nooks and crannies, picturesque pro-
files"—in a sarcastic way to describe the friendly and thoughtful
elements of domestic design employed by the architects of Alton East,
and as if there were no difference between these and the genuinely tacky
detailing of much artless modern private housing.[19] Here again, then,
sentiment was sought out and blasted by ridicule. This is how losers are
identified and eliminated: through show trials based on unfair and irrelevant comparisons. "Flimsy . . . Effeminate": in 1976 Reyner Banham,
champion of "The New Brutalism," quoted with relish these words
written twenty-five years beforehand by Lionel Brett; they had been
intended by their original author to convey bemused appreciation of the
Scandinavianist, funfair architecture of the Festival of Britain, but they
were deployed by Banham to highlight what looked to him then like a

derivative overrated mishmash, a worn-out, feeble, populist style; only
the landscaping was any good, he said, and only he had noticed it: a
bizarre show-off comment typical of Brutalist dismissiveness.[20]

In the case of the late Jan Kaplický of the architectural practice
Future Systems, architects and writers seemed to pile in on top of each
other to be rude about his work, in the letters columns of magazines as
well as in critical articles. The *Architectural Review*, which during Peter
Davey's editorship firmly disapproved of gratuitous formalism,
described Kaplický's Selfridges store in Birmingham as an "outrage"
and a "a blue blancmange with chickenpox," but this was mild compared to a comment from an architect and former Royal Institute of
British Architects Council member who, according to the *Architects'
Journal*, called for the council to "pull [Selfridges] down and start
again" because it appeared to contravene a natural lighting regulation.[21]
For one architect to call for the demolition of the work of another
because of a relatively minor technical problem is rudeness at its worst.
The critic Kieran Long, writing in a magazine called *Icon*, which sees
itself as a fashion leader, deployed metropolitan sneering: Kaplický's
building was a "blob, a strange juxtaposition of supposedly cutting-
edge architecture and marketing that already looks dreadfully out of
date."[22] *Building Design* chose to report two years later that even the
head of retail development at the rival department store John Lewis—a
company that has prided itself for generations on its friendly image—
managed to throw in an insult at Selfridges' "theatricality" and its dubious approach to "sustainability."[23] Kaplický's battle to realize his project
for a new national library in Prague may have contributed to his premature death in 2009: in an obituary notice, Damian Arnold wrote
that "the strain of fighting for the project is said to have taken its toll."[24]
It is possible that bullying or humiliation also goes on within architects'
offices in ways that the principals are not necessarily even aware of.
Some people have a horror of being asked to participate in physical
activities—ones which for example require them to wear shorts in front
of the people they work with in order to play sports with them, or to
otherwise demonstrate physical stamina or competitive instincts which
they might not have. The opportunity to get down on a mat and engage
with colleagues in a bout of judo, once offered by Edward Cullinan's
office, might not have been every architect's idea of practice.[25]

No one is any wiser about any kind of architecture as a result of writing and speaking about it in aggressive tones; defenses close in, sides are taken, and the great majority of new architecture fails to develop in an interesting way because the publications that architects and their teachers read have no real means of speaking about it and describing it. Some architecture critics invent fake emotions, perhaps evoking some tragic grandeur in a coarse, overscaled building, because they are unable to confront the real, human ones involved. We are all aware, all too often, that a building apparently needs to break some visual barrier or perpetrate an aesthetic outrage of some kind to be worthy of attention. When a building does none of these things—and that is to say, in fact, nearly all of them—architecture critics are reduced either to writing dry descriptions or to talking about vague ideas that are supposedly lodged in the heads of designers.[26] In a recent interview with Chris Foges, the editor of *Architecture Today*, Meades berated architecture critics for their old-fashioned, narrow way of writing about buildings:

> A lot of architectural writing, particularly in the broadsheets, takes buildings as stand-alone events, staged by David Chipperfield or Milords Foster or Rogers, and treats them as art objects; it has nothing to do with anyone's experience.[27]

Why?

VIRILE / FLIMSY AND EFFEMINATE

Virility: this was the word used approvingly by the *Architects' Journal* to describe Mendelsohn's Bexhill Pavilion as compared to the shortlisted entries for the contemporary new town hall for the London borough of Hackney, all of which were neoclassical. The search for virility has blighted architectural criticism. Why should anyone want it here? Is there any connection with making children? With showing off in the gym? What is its role and purpose in the design of buildings?

Architecture makes plenty of valid appearances in the worlds of the flimsy, the effeminate, and the sentimental, created by other types of artist; the way in which it is treated there tells us something about what is missing from conventional criticism. While Le Corbusier was busy praising the virility of engineers, a novelist who lived in seclusion in the Lake District was writing bestselling books which provide a window onto how architecture was seen by people who were not architects—and indeed no doubt also by some loser-architects who were mired in that great vice of "sentimentality." From 1930 Hugh Walpole, a popular writer, speaker, and raconteur who is almost completely forgotten now, wrote a sequence of novels collectively entitled *Rogue Herries*, after the first book of the series, which follow the lives of members of a rural family across centuries of English history. The parts of this that interest me are Walpole's descriptions of life and architecture from the reign of Queen Anne which appear in the first novel, both because they reflect a current trend in fashionable design—and a victim of the brutality of the virile critics—but also because they continue a notable theme that had been appearing in literature elsewhere.

Before taking this further, we need to look into the connotations of the words "Queen Anne." They have a particular power to them in architecture, like that accorded to "Victorian," but more sophisticated in meaning than the latter. The real domestic architecture of Queen Anne, who reigned from 1702 to 1714, was for the greater part not truly distinguishable from the late Stuart architecture that preceded it and the Georgian architecture that immediately followed it—at its best, you can identify it by good-quality brickwork, a relatively large proportion of wall to window, deep timber eaves, exposed sash-window counterweight boxes, and ornamental doorcases. The building of St. Paul's Cathedral continued throughout the queen's reign, and some of Christopher Wren's other monuments, Nicholas Hawksmoor's London churches, and the great houses of John Vanbrugh are the buildings that lend the period true distinction. When "Queen Anne" was adopted as the name of a style in the latter part of the nineteenth century, the houses described as such did not really match the real thing from a century and a half earlier. The first "Queen Anne" house of the Victorian period is often said to be that erected in Kensington by the novelist W. M. Thackeray, the author of *Vanity Fair* and much else, apparently to his own design with the help of the architect Frederick Hering in 1860. It looked like an attempt at a Wren style, possibly as a result of the insistence of the Crown Commissioners (who owned the site) on a building that would complement Wren's Kensington Palace opposite; but it suited Thackeray too, because he was an enthusiast for the eighteenth century, which he popularized through his novels.[28] George Gilbert Scott junior—who lived in a genuine Queen Anne house in Hampstead, and was once photographed dressed in a Queen Anne-period outfit—seems to have expressed his defiance toward his father's strictly Gothic practice by taking up the style some ten years later. This younger Scott, an "architects' architect," was widely admired by contemporaries, and others followed his lead. In particular the young stars of the arts and crafts movement who had emerged from the office of Richard Norman Shaw began to experiment with loose and unhistorical compositions of sliding sash windows and brick ornament, the latter often in carved panels, expensive, delicate work; the interiors included much polished, rather than varnished, timber, and ornaments in ceramics and plain metals. The results did not much resemble the far stiffer buildings of the period of the real Queen Anne, but the name stuck. By the time "Queen Anne" emerged as a label in the United States, it referred to a distant cousin of the English versions: it means the ahistorical end-of-century style characterized by ornamental, usually curved timberwork; tiles, colored glass and fancy fireplaces, the predecessor of the Shingle Style. Mark Girouard's book *Sweetness and Light* summarizes what the late-Victorian "Queen Anne" was about: it was a reaction to the heaviness of high-Victorian architecture and interior design, and its arrival coincided with a fashion for Georgiana in the drawings of Randolph Caldecott and Kate Greenaway—children's illustrators, of course. Girouard also points out that the initial professional reaction to the new "Queen Anne" was one of virulent derision, but that the public generally liked it, evidently a rare example of an avant-garde, artistic style of architecture pleasing the latter before the former; and by the end of the century the style had acquired something of the warm, friendly character of the Tudor and Elizabethan revivals that had followed Walter Scott.[29]

But whereas the Tudor and Elizabethan revivals had been blasted to bits by the Gothic Revival, "Queen Anne" made a sideways move once the high-art people had become bored with it. By the beginning of the twentieth century it was turning into a delicate hybrid style that mixed the early-eighteenth-century with details chosen from the Regency domestic architecture of about a century later: bow windows, tripartite vertical sliding sash windows, ornamental wrought iron work. The appearance of this phenomenon coincides with a revival in interest in the same period by writers and artists. J. M. Barrie, for example, wrote in 1901 a popular and successful play called *Quality Street* about a genteel young lady called Miss Phoebe Throssell going about her business—card games, shopping trips, exciting young men—in a country town. Lutyens designed the original stage sets for it, and a 1913 book edition featured charming drawings by Hugh Thomson, an illustrator who had taken over where Caldecott left off. In fact the phenomenon as a whole might be called "Quality Street"—a wistful yearning for an age of delicate architecture that had been exterminated by the High Gothic Revival, with its moral strictures and material vulgarity.

FIGURE 3.3
"Miss Fanny is reading aloud from a library book while the others sew or knit." One of Hugh Thomson's illustrations for a 1913 edition of J. M. Barrie's *Quality Street*.

FIGURE 3.4
The Quality Street style combined early-
eighteenth-century forms with Regency-
era detailing. This is the "sedan-chair"
back door at Horace Field's *Church Times*
office block in London (1904). Courtesy
of the author.

At the beginning of the twentieth century, our loser Horace Field
was for a period a Quality Street architect *par excellence*. The large newspaper and publisher's building he designed off London's Kingsway even
has a sedan chair entrance round the back. At the other end of the scale,
he made the most of wartime restrictions on new building in 1916 by
remodeling a row of plain Victorian shops in the town of Farnham in
Surrey into an idealized Quality Street-type shopping parade, actually
camouflage for a new branch of Lloyds Bank; he placed an unexpected
row of Tuscan pillars inside, and one can almost see Barrie's Miss
Phoebe chatting to a matron or a subaltern alongside them. A well-
known polemical book of 1928 by Clough Williams-Ellis called *England and the Octopus*, a condemnation of post-First World War urban
sprawl, illustrated the shop fronts as an example of what a town center
parade should look like, but failed to give Field, by then in terminal
professional decline, any credit for it, another way in which Field found
himself a loser; and yet presumably Williams-Ellis had realized that
these were not genuinely old façades.[30]

This was effeminate architecture; and over the years that followed it
made friends with an increasingly homoerotic strain in English literature.
At first the new hybrid version of "Queen Anne" simply meant calmness,

FIGURE 3.5
Quality Street-style shop fronts added in 1916 by Horace Field to plain Victorian
buildings in the Surrey town of Farnham. Courtesy of Keith Diplock.

retiral, serenity. That is how it appears when the novelist H. G. Wells
deploys it, for example in his novels *Kipps* of 1905 and *The History of
Mr Polly* of five years later, in both cases making a reference to the
picturesque town of Rye in Sussex. In 1925 Field built one of his unso-
phisticated neo-Georgian houses here, cheap and plain compared to
the work of his prime, a kind of empty dolls' house, for two sisters who,
according to their biographer, loved "beautiful places, beautiful things
in simplicity and good order."[31] He also converted Chatwin's ugly bank
branch in the town center into a masterpiece of the style, and received
the plaudits of the council for doing so.[32] The town was a kind of
national capital for Quality Street—for evidence you need only look at
all the good-taste memorials to Hampstead artists in its parish church.
It is not surprising, therefore, that Rye became the setting for E. F.
Benson's extremely camp *Mapp and Lucia* stories, comedies about two
bossy middle-class women with social and artistic pretensions who are
surrounded by emasculated, infantilized, probably homosexual men,
and are full of praise for "Queen Anne": "What a wonderful time, Pope
and Addison! So civilized, so cultivated!"[33]

I would say that Field was this time actually in the vanguard of a new movement that was to continue through to the 1950s rather than being, as first appears retrospectively after years of modernist history writing, a failure stuck in an old one. For the fascinating thing is that it was exactly at this moment that the hybrid-"Queen Anne" style suddenly took off in popular English culture, and remained there in some places right until after the Second World War. As the architect Paul Paget put it, looking back at the mid-1920s from his retirement, "to be classy—to be intelligent—you had to like Georgian and that was that"; he was referring to young architects from his own social circle, upper- and upper-middle-class, sociable, cocktail-party, formal-dinner people, the classiest of whom was Gerald Wellesley, the bisexual future 7th Duke of Wellington.[34] Books over the last thirty years, usually emanating from the stalwarts of the architectural amenity societies, or of the Royal Institute of British Architects collection, are finally beginning to build up a more representative picture of this type of architecture, but it has otherwise been completely ignored in conventional pan-century narratives.[35] The evidence for the rise of "Queen Anne" at this time can be seen all over the place—in architecture, in the wholesale adoption of Field's style for thousands of bank branches, post offices, tea rooms (especially), dress shops, and much else across the country; in theater and set design, and period films such as *Me and Marlborough* (1935); in home décor; and of course in popular novels, and in a range of confectionery called "Quality Street" which until recently came in gift boxes and tins decorated with Regency characters, and at one point was sold from a "Queen Anne"-style shop in the center of York.[36]

One of the places this tendency lasted a long time, and from a late start, has been in the popular series of Superquick cardboard models of houses that train enthusiasts, usually retired and male, still use to decorate their train sets. These were designed from 1960 onward by a commercial artist called Donovan Lloyd in what the current proprietors of the company informally call the "Basingstoke 1935" style, meaning that they are intended to reflect the comfortable high street of the interwar period in the prosperous areas around London; they include, for example, a group called "Regency House and Shops." The models are still in production, and Lloyd's attempts to modernize them by including 1960s-style buildings proved unpopular, specifically among the people from the tidy, obsessive, and yet romantic world of the miniature railway modelers who themselves are still longing for the age of the steam locomotive that they can now only just remember.[37] Something in the Quality Street style evidently struck a chord in many people beyond the architectural profession. Another place where it made an appearance, in the early 1950s, was in the volumes of the *Daily Mail*'s popular *Ideal Home Book*, annuals which accompanied the newspaper's Ideal Home Exhibition in London, which for a period around the queen's coronation in 1953 were full of "Regency" wallpapers, furniture, and knickknacks.

It must surely be its unreal delicacy that made the style all the more attractive in the interwar age with its morbid fears, or in the postwar era when so much was uncertain, or unrecognizable, or in ruins. It seems logical that architects of these tumultuous periods should want to cling on to the Regency as they might want to cling on to a disappearing childhood, knowing, likewise, that this had been a style that was fated to die. The ultimate illustration of the period for me is James Durden's *Summer in Cumberland* (1925), in which a boy in cricket whites stands outside a Queen Anneian Palladian window, looking in as his mother and sister sit at a table laid with a white cloth and a silver tea service.[38] Here one feels on one's skin the dappled light, the buttery glow of the painted room, the distant view of the hills, the flutter of the cut flowers

FIGURE 3.6
Cardboard "Regency" façade kits for railway modelers, designed by Donovan Lloyd for Superquick in the 1960s. By kind permission of Superquick Models (PEMS Butler Ltd.).

within and the trees without. The significance for me is that the artist has perpetuated a scene which, while perfect, is transient, will come apart and never come back, more so than is the case in most genre painting. This boy, as a painted figure, will never reach his sex-hungry twenties; this mother will never grow old and frail; this sister will never be sold to a loveless husband. The attraction is that transience, that fleeting grasp at something beautiful, something that is gone, something which belonged to someone else anyway. It is the only picture I have ever wanted to be in. If a number of people, the satirist and cartoonist Osbert Lancaster among them, thought of the revived Regency style as a kind of reboot from where architecture had arrived at before the Gothic Revival savaged it, it must surely for others have been a style of failure, one whose future annihilation was perpetually awaiting it in the wings.[39]

This is where the novelist Hugh Walpole comes in. It is easy to see why the Herries novels were such a hit: it happens surprisingly often in them that people are spanking or splashing each other, or stripping off

FIGURE 3.7
Summer in Cumberland, by James Durden (1925). Courtesy of Manchester City Galleries.

their own clothes or other people's, usually in or near the Herries family's rugged rural retreat in the wilds of the Lake District. A great deal of the story's popular appeal lay, no doubt, in the continued and manipulative contrast Walpole drew between this and the other aesthetic experience of the novels, the pleasant architecture and life of the genteel people whom Herries encounters—for Walpole had latched onto Queen Anne as a form of shorthand for gentility and elegance, everything that rough Herries world was not. A typical example runs:

> This modern world so novel, strident, ill-fitting. . . . And (here his Herries blood drove him) he disliked and distrusted this modernity. Queen Anne's age appeared to him as something infinitely quiet, cosy, picturesque and easy.[40]

Elsewhere, an affectionate old bachelor uncle who loves the opera, and "has a way with young men," is described as "an old dreamer and babbles of Queen Anne," and there is also an architect who "spoke in a shrill piping voice, and trembled with anger, so they said, at the sight of a woman."[41]

There cannot be anything realistic here. I may be wrong, but I do not think a Lakeland farmer in the mid-eighteenth century would have fantasized about a style of décor from thirty years beforehand, and so it seems that the novelist is conveying something else, most likely about himself and the times he is living in. *Rogue Herries* is not a subtle book, and the use of Queen Anne is explicit. It is presented as the architectural style of those who have retired from the aggressive masculinity and morbidity of real life, in the mid-eighteenth century as much as in 1930, and used to give a more explicitly homoerotic character to the earthy parts of the story through simple contrasts: spanking boys in the fields; sipping tea in Queen Anne parlors.[42] This is a specifically gay escapism, with considerably more emphasis on the men, undisciplined, unruly, and the boys, their bodies and their actions, than on the women, all of whom are less well developed as characters. The story of Walpole's own life would seem to make this a plausible reading.[43] What I am saying here is that this popular novel, which does not appear to be about architecture, in fact has a great deal to say about it through the few lines dedicated to it within its pages: the descriptions of the

Queen Anne style are relatively well developed and consistent in relation to other descriptive sections, and integral to the plot in the sense
that one needs to understand these houses and interiors in order to
gauge the character of their inhabitants, or what passes through the
minds of those who visit there. The period décor in *Rogue Herries*, and
in the films and interior design magazines of the era, are explicit examples of a phenomenon across the 1920s and 1930s in which unconven-
tional people are trying to re-create for a new and unsettled period in
their lives the type of interior décor they would like to have had in the
first place, in the dream version of their own youth or childhood: the
architecture of self-infantilization and retrenchment. If you were Walpole, born in the 1880s—the son of a churchman in New Zealand—you
would have grown up with an entirely different sort of interior from
those he depicted in his novels. If Alan Hollinghurst presents the architectural significance of "Two Acres" through sensitive, arch hints, then
Walpole, addressing a much more general and larger audience, presents
his slightly more coherent pictures of imaginary houses as provocative
and almost defiant in relation to the norms of his times, explaining
without the pretension and elevated tools of an architecture critic exactly
how and why buildings are important to a story. In fact it seems to me
that Walpole described the appeal of Queen Anne houses rather better
than any of the architectural writers at the time managed to do.

This is a book for sissies, then, and it deploys Queen Anne architecture because that was the architecture of sissies—not of the polemicists; not of the Bauhaus or of Le Corbusier; not even of the *Architects'
Journal* (after 1935, at least); it is the architecture of amateurism, of
sentimentality. It is a kind of architecture where discussion is genteel
and quite unrelated to concepts. It is reassuring, warm; cozy; well-pol-
ished, predictable. As is often the case with gay phenomena in culture,
it rapidly spread: The architectural magazines were full of it; even the
cover of the *Architectural Review* with its elegant captions that resem-
bled eighteenth-century script was part of it, evidence that it had considerable allure for the high-art people too. Yet British architectural
history has nothing to say about the entire phenomenon of Quality
Street and still very little to say about the Regency revival, even if
American history, being by and large more catholic, more generous,
and perhaps less homophobic, has a little more.

A COUPLE OF SISSIE ARCHITECTS

It is now possible to reconstruct a great deal about interwar neo-Georgian architecture both from the copious literature of the period—books by capable designers about what they saw as good design for shops and shop fronts—and from recent scholarship in journals such as that of the Twentieth Century Society, the British amenity group. But none of these attempts to give any interpretation of the style beyond description, and buildings are by and large characterized in terms of being "good" or "indifferent" examples. Looking at some of these specifically architectural stories differently can indicate how much is being missed. A good example is that of the British partnership of Seely and Paget. They produced one masterpiece and a large number of other buildings for prestigious institutions, including churches for the diocese of London during the period after the Second World War when they were the diocesan architects and surveyors to the fabric of St. Paul's Cathedral; but to date there is nothing that tells their story as a whole, probably because their buildings were relentlessly indifferent compared to those that we all remember from the period.

John Seely, the son of a politician whose later career was blighted by his having been an appeaser and an apologist for Hitler, took a degree in architecture at Cambridge from 1919 to 1922 and was the partnership's designer; Paul Paget, on the other hand, had no design training at all, nor any ability to design. He met Seely when they were both undergraduates at Trinity College, Cambridge, and quickly formed a deep bond—"we became virtually one person," as he put it—and the two established their practice in a pretty and genuine Queen Anne house and street (*circa* 1705) in Westminster immediately after Seely's graduation. They lived and worked together until death separated them, and friends and family called them "The Partners."[44] Paget's job was to run the office and answer the telephone, and he charmed clients and potential clients. In the words of his stepson, he liked everything about being an architect—attending their clubs, openings, parties and exhibitions, and handling models, and so on—except the actual process of design, in which he took no part.[45] And no doubt the parties and the rest of it were agreeable events, because both Seely and Paget were well connected through their families to influential people and institutions which quickly provided them with a great deal of work. Their first project involved some remodeling for the well-known actress Gladys Cooper at her house in Highgate, north London, and soon afterward there followed a similar job next door for the future novelist and playwright J. B. Priestley—who, incidentally, was in 1948 to publish a beautiful little piece of late Quality Street drama, *The High Toby*, with set and costume designs by Doris Zinkeisen, for Pollock's Toy Theatres. "I mean you were just introduced to the right people, behaved in the right way, and so commission followed commission," as Paget much later recalled to Clive Aslet.[46] The one feature of their architecture which has passed into legend is the double bathroom—two tubs, side by side—at their own pre-Great-Fire timber house at 41 Cloth Fair in the City of London. They subsequently bought and refurbished several other houses in the same street, apparently with the intention of maintaining an idealized streetscape, and after the Second World War they restored the bomb-damaged Charterhouse nearby. They also designed and built a summer house for themselves on the Isle of Wight estate of the Seely family; here they sat and drank cocoa in the evening, and slept one above the other in bunk beds.[47]

Their one masterpiece is their restoration and new building in 1933–1936 at Eltham Palace, a splendid fifteenth-century hall to the southeast of London which had fallen into disrepair. The additions, for the wealthy Courtauld textile family, turned the hall into the centerpiece of a mansion in an unusual (for England) domestic, brown-brick version of the early French château style, stage-set Henri Quatre. It is the inside, however, that is not only celebrated but seen more often than one might think; it includes a triangular hall which makes frequent appearances in television and film dramas set in the 1930s, immediately recognizable by the marquetry panels depicting Rome and Stockholm around its walls, which recall Williams-Ellis's remark: "unless you are really rich, it is wise to be born an Italian or a Scandinavian."[48] This interior of this room was designed by the Swedish designer Rolf Engströmer, and the imposing Art Deco-classical dining room by Peter Malacrida; the "Italian Drawing Room," also by Malacrida, was a showpiece of the style that was dubbed by Lancaster "Curzon Street Baroque," a style employing pieces of ornamental ironwork from Spanish churches that were then to be found in the antique shops of London's Mayfair.[49]

Seely and Paget never again pulled off so comprehensive and successful a building as they did at Eltham, and even then their triumph was
shared with the interior designers. The building's fame is mostly due in
any case to its interiors; the outside was described by one writer as resem-
bling "an admirably designed but unfortunately sited cigarette factory."[50]
When they worked on historical buildings—for example, during postwar
restorations of damaged structures around Westminster Abbey, Eton
College, and the ancient King's School, Canterbury—they designed in a
simplified, cheapened version of the style of the original buildings, often
(in reconstruction) a weak "Queen Anne." Many of their postwar churches
were simple brick boxes. One of them, St. Mary's West Kensington,
London, sits at the end of the street I grew up in, and I remember it
only as a pleasant but plain structure with a slightly decorative tower

FIGURE 3.8
Eltham Palace, in south London, designed by Seely
and Paget in 1933–1936: the highlight of their
career. Courtesy of English Heritage Photo Library.

and pinnacle. I get the feeling, looking now at photographs of the work of Seely and Paget, that they liked sticking slightly decorative things onto or around a plain building; some of these decorative things took the form of an overbold and unattractive overscaled expressed structural frame. Near Holborn Circus, at the boundary of the City of London, they produced a building like this when they restored a damaged church, with peculiar and unsatisfactory results, although they made more of a success of the same idea when they designed the parish church for the first New Town of Stevenage.[51]

One of the interesting facts about Seely and Paget is that they built up a substantial practice and reputation through working in no definable style, rather in the way that some celebrities seem to make a career out of being celebrities. It is quite possible to be a good architect in a challenging and austere period using an indefinable style of bricks and concrete frames: George Pace, a church architect a little younger than Seely and Paget, was just that, bringing traces of Gio Ponti to provincial England. But neither the trained Seely nor the untrained Paget had any talent for designing. When Seely died, at the comparatively early age of 61, Paget had the grace to resign the surveyorship of St. Paul's Cathedral, knowing that he was not capable of doing it on his own. He finally troubled himself to travel to Italy for the first time, and then retired to Templewood, the camp, beautiful little pavilion the partnership had built in Norfolk for his uncle in 1938 which incorporated parts from two recently demolished major neoclassical buildings, Nuthall Temple and the Bank of England. Paget decorated its single large splendid room with a ceiling mural in Tiepolo style by Brian Thomas which depicts glorified versions of his young self, for example posing as a schoolboy athlete, although in reality he had always been hopeless at sports. There is a vast number of documents and drawings from the partnership in the collection of the Royal Institute of British Architects, but it seems unlikely that anyone will want to spend the time required going through it all. If it were moved into a library for the studies of masculinity and gender there might be a better chance of that, because the story of Seely and Paget is primarily one of a strong partnership between two teenagers who wanted to grow up together and do things together. This is what the story is about, I think, and how this played a role in mid-twentieth-century modern life. Paget waited for eight years after Seely's death before marrying for the first time at the age of seventy. Seely and Paget were the sissie architects about whom no conventional architectural historian has so far thought of anything to say.

Some architects form groups that seem to have been bonded together by homosexuality, and in some cases by failure too. Clive Aslet, one of the few writers whose work evokes the full story of the buildings he discusses, says that everything to do with the homosexual Charles Ashbee and his various endeavors was marked by failure, from his attempts at founding a living-working artists' community (with nude river bathing, music playing, hopeless economics, and so on) in the Cotswolds, to his work for the doomed Earl Beauchamp at Madresfield, the latter a clear example of a house haunted by what he calls "the suggestion of failure and even tragedy that befell so many Arts and Crafts undertakings."[52] I wonder whether homosexuals who did much of the work for major architects were particularly prone to loserdom—possibly for example Joseph Wells, the first principal designer of McKim, Mead and White; and some of the ghost designers for Philip Johnson's practice, or in his circle: John Bedenkapp and Peter van der Meulen Smith, for example.[53] It is not surprising that the bullies can identify the sissies who may in some cases be in explicitly homosexual groups, and then set out to crush them. Of course, some well-known homosexual architects have themselves been quite good at bullying; but surely for much of the twentieth century most were bullied and lonely people, and their response to their condition may have been to try to design themselves into a more beautiful world: that is, a sentimental one. In the interwar period that tendency may have been further exaggerated by a more general "morbid" response—to use the historian Richard Overy's word—to the apparently catastrophic condition of Europe and America, and the ugliness and squalor of the cities and the poor that must have seemed beyond redemption.[54] And in England, in any case, it was until recently by no means unusual for any people with an interest in the arts to be treated *as if they were* homosexuals. As Bryan Appleyard put it in his biography of the unmistakably heterosexual Richard Rogers, already living and sleeping with his girlfriend at the age of fourteen, his school's hearty, healthy brew of sport, hard work and bracing spirituality broadly categorized the sort of artistic sensitivity that Rogers was absorbing from Dada [his father] as something to do with homosexuality.[55]

THE "BEAUTIE OF HOLINESSE"

As a group, evangelical Christians are capable of an almost unsurpassed bullying of homosexuals and sissies in general; and evangelical attitudes to church architecture and interiors are likewise bullying to an extent that goes beyond threat to actual aggression. Presumably, like Rogers's teachers, they think that the two are related, and that sensibility to the visual arts marks a person out as being insufficiently manly. This has a long history to it, as the organized destruction of church art at various points in history continuously testifies, from the Reformation to the English Civil War and Commonwealth—and it continues now in England, after an evangelical minister has taken over a church which still has surviving Victorian artifacts in it. The handbook used by evangelicals, described on its cover as "the definitive guide to re-ordering church buildings for worship and mission," and much reissued, is called *Re-pitching the Tent*. It was first published in 1996 and written by Richard Giles, a priest with a record of remodeling churches in both Britain and the United States.

Giles's book tells you how it is done: something called "Victorian clutter" is removed, which means just about everything, and new and cheap furniture is put in its place. Facing the start of a chapter called "Our Mobilisation" there is a full-page illustration of a Gothic church being demolished, while the vandalistic churchgoers hurry joyously to a new, ugly, shedlike building in the distance, rather like one of Pugin's illustrations in his *Contrasts* but intended to make the opposite point.[56] In fact Giles deploys a Puginian trick when he compares views of Wren's St. Stephen's, Walbrook, in the City of London before and after recent reordering: the former is depicted in a dull black-and-white photograph, the latter flatteringly in color.[57]

Gleeful destruction is all around in *Re-pitching the Tent*. One story told in the book explains how a congregation recorded the "history" of their building by leaving the scar formed when a Victorian pulpit was removed rather than having the stonework restored.[58] That looks to me like sadism. In the United States Giles oversaw, as dean, the reordering of the Episcopal cathedral in Philadelphia, which consisted of the removal of its historical artifacts and murals and the insertion of fewer, cheaper and less long-lasting replacements. This process caused some friction at the time; Roger W. Moss, the historian of Philadelphia's places of worship, questioned the "wanton destruction" of the building's earlier rich decorative scheme, and pointed out that other reordered churches had managed a reasonable degree of compromise; he asked whether the Giles scheme was simply "insensitive vandalism sanctimoniously cloaking itself, in the dean's words, with a 'conviction that the mission of the Church should always take precedence whenever architectural layout conflicts with the Church's current needs in liturgy or ministry'," a bold phrase that stands out in a book otherwise written in notably diplomatic and sympathetic language.[59] The new scheme and the terms used to defend it were, to me, an example of architectural bullying, perhaps aimed at aesthetes whose priorities are, quite simply, not important to busy, "virile" people. And bullies are not satisfied with just removing a pew here and there. In 2006 the British government tried to demolish Robert Matthew, Johnson-Marshall & Partners' beautiful Commonwealth Institute in Kensington, that gorgeous cadmium-blue butterfly I loved so much as a child, which sits on state land, with the argument that starving children in Africa would die unless the site was sold to support the government's international aid program.[60]

It always astonishes me that even the waste of good materials does not bother these people. As a member of the Victorian Society committee which considers applications to alter buildings listed for their architectural or historical merit in the south of England, I see time and time again cases where a minister responds angrily to the charge that he is destroying the long-term heritage of his church by telling us that this is what God, or Jesus, wants him to do. God has asked him, for example, to replace a fine oak door on wrought-iron hinges with a glass one so that passersby can look through and be "welcomed" in (these makeshift glass porches are sometimes called "Welcome Doors" on their architects' drawings); or to smash up or sell "inflexible" Victorian benches, as if God didn't know any more than the vicar that a glass door will reflect the sunlight outside rather than allowing a view in, or that the churchgoers, having removed their Victorian benches, will not actually bother to rearrange their replacement plastic chairs as one year follows the next. Or that God didn't know any more than they did that the artifacts of religious culture are also the memorials of those who made them, the only kind of lasting memorial those mainly forgotten people, with their hard lives, are likely to achieve.

A recurring feature of these applications is the provision of lavatories for visitors, inside or directly attached to a historic, even medieval, building, even when it would be perfectly possible and reasonable to allow these to be located at a manageable distance from the old one. It turns out that the prominent and intrusive provision of water closets is an article of faith—literally—for evangelical Anglicans. Following a discussion on one of these applications, I Googled the local vicar, not least because his name was familiar as someone I had shared a staircase with as a university undergraduate, and I found a recording of a sermon he had given in Peterborough, Cambridgeshire, in a church at the extreme end of the British ultra-evangelical spectrum. Very soon he launched into this favored aspect of architecture, perhaps the only one that these people find interesting.

The message I understood from the vicar's address was that it was a matter of principle not to accord the fabric of the church building, however venerable or beautiful, any kind of priority over the practical needs of the congregation. The fact that mainstream or High Church Anglicans do not add lavatories within the aisles or even the naves of their ancient churches, and seem to revere their accumulated historical contents, in particular their "Victorian clutter," is apparently a sign that they prefer buildings to people. The vicar was valiantly fighting against any suggestion that people and the structures they inhabit or use often share a common narrative—the one thing that is needed for people who are not architects if they are to value and talk about buildings. I would have thought that the insistence on the prominence of an ugly block containing many lavatories at considerable cost to the aesthetics and completeness of a sacred building showed an almost psychotic hatred of beauty, not to mention a nasty tendency to bully both a building and those who valued it. Looking back at Anglican history, it seems clear that the Puritan assault on Archbishop Laud's attempts at beautifying churches despoiled at the Reformation—the "beautie of holinesse," as it is sometimes called—was at least as much an act of aesthetic bullying as the political and theological attack it is generally made out to be. And "Victorian clutter" is in any case a subjective and misleading term, deployed as tendentious propaganda. As Tom Ashley, the Churches Conservation Adviser of the Victorian Society, recently put it, when describing the intended despoliation of yet another fine medieval and Victorian church by an evangelical congregation, the neat lines of Victorian benches usually contribute order and repose to a space, whereas the curved rows of moveable chairs preferred by evangelicals, which often cut through the nave and aisles without any reference to the axial rectangularity of their spaces or even of their massive stone piers, are disruptive and disturbing.[61] So what ought to be a discussion about architecture, its associations and its stories, its beauties and its dreams, turns into some kind of a sermon about lavatories and chairs. This is what I see time and time again from my membership of the committee: England's beautiful medieval churches, sometimes restored and furnished by Victorians to what were then the highest standards of design and craftsmanship in the world, continually under threat of vandalization and mutilation by a here-today, gone-tomorrow priest; they are soon filled with cheap tiles, cheap carpets, cheap furniture; cheap everything. It is true that talking to bullies is always difficult, but this situation is the consequence of there being no adequate common language for talking about everyday things in architecture.

SLIDING INTO HOPELESSNESS

I am going to stay for a moment longer on the subject of churches, and use it as a bridge between the perpetual losing battle between the bullies and the sissies, and the next chapter, on hopelessness. I am looking now at a rather glum book, recent but with black-and-white photographs, which is a gazetteer of churches built for the Church of England in London between the two world wars. Few churches were in fact built until the 1930s; then the Church experienced one of its short booms in activity, a boom which—like a later and similar one in the

1950s—soon fizzled out.[62] A handful of these interwar churches are the work of great designers: they include Edward Maufe's church of St. Thomas, Hanwell, a masterful sculpted brick composition in the suburbs of London that was evidently considered progressive enough to have made it into the newly modern *Architects' Journal* in 1935; Maufe also produced the smaller St. Saviour, Acton; and Giles Gilbert Scott, like Maufe a cathedral designer, built St. Alban, Golders Green, not one of his more memorable designs. These winners' buildings make only slight reference to a historical style, and their impact as buildings derives from the emphasis their architects placed on the general sculptural form of the buildings and their white walls, good sculpture and brickwork; if anything they are slightly Byzantine in appearance. There are also two good expressionist churches by N. F. Cachemaille-Day, Britain's unrecognized answer to Fritz Höger and a loser, I think, given the lack of interest in and the physical condition of his churches today; and a gaunt basilica by Adshead & Ramsey, for some reason not in the same neo-Regency style as the architects' Duchy of Cornwall estate in Kennington nearby. But pretty much all the rest of the buildings are disappointing failures. Some 1920s Gothic buildings are reasonable, if somewhat on the cheap side; some are stretched-out, washed-out Victoriana; some already have a cheapskate feel about them; some were conceived on a grand scale but never finished. Many of the others look like cinemas; there is a characteristic one in Tottenham, north London, by Seely and Paget, that for me still says "the weekend is over," because I used to pass it in the car when my aunt was driving me back into London on Sunday evening, ready to go off to school the following morning. It is fronted by a semicircular portico which is one of their "decorative things," here attached to a block that looks as if it ought to be a gymnasium, very peculiar and clumsy (or, in the understated words of the book's authors, "rather odd").

But the great majority are in no particular style: perhaps they are a little Byzantine, a little Tudorish, or in a cheap or thin Gothic: they could almost provide an updated illustration for the buildings derided in Pugin's *True Principles*, or *An Apology*. Milner & Craze, mainly well known (if at all) for having disappointingly rebuilt Pugin's St. George's Cathedral, Southwark, south London, after serious bomb damage in the Second World War, and the awkward, Spanish-looking (almost)

FIGURE 3.9
The Church of St. John the Baptist, Tottenham, north
London, by Seely and Paget (1940): more typical of the
greater part of their output. Courtesy of Keith Diplock.

High Anglican shrine at Walsingham in flat and cold Norfolk, appear
here as the authors of two churches within the same borough: the first
in a curious pre-Pugin Gothic style, the second in no style whatsoever.
The Gothic Revival, for all its bombast, did manage to establish a
common, understandable language for the architecture of churches; the
Church of England, in decline after the First World War, found none.
Thus these buildings seem to sum up the failed achievements of the
era, worth nothing to conventional historians. What this little book
provides, then, is a window into an area of hopelessness, a great
endeavor to build churches for the established church in the metropo-
lis, which ended up with a collection of buildings of dubious quality,
nearly all sissies, buildings to be laughed at for their feebleness of style,

all presented through unprepossessing amateur black-and-white photography with little contrast, all of which adds to the sense of futility of the buildings and even, in turn, of the project of looking at them and recording them. I am delighted to say that the authors have now published a successor volume on the new London churches of the postwar period. After all, as all loser and winner architects know, there is nothing like wasting one's time reading or writing a book when there is something more masculine that is waiting to be designed and built out there somewhere.

HOPELESSNESS

WHAT IS IT REALLY ABOUT?

This is a chapter about some other ways in which designers can fail to achieve the thing they are dreaming of when they set out to create a building, and about how the hopelessness of a project from the outset and the disappointment with its outcome can turn out to be the most interesting things about it. No doubt many of the churches we heard about in chapter 3, especially the unfinished ones, carry the traces of fascinating stories. For me these buildings represent together the height of aspiration but also the disappointment of their realization, the giving birth by the architect to a malformed child. They can set off a little series of explosions—a chain reaction of one disaster after the next—the more one looks into them, each one carrying, like sad comets, a trail of stories in their wake.

At a road junction a few minutes' drive from my house there is a small evangelical Anglican church called St. Mark's, located on a large and mostly empty site. You will doubtless be able to find something similar near you. What originally drew my attention was the tall but narrow block with arched windows, built from red-brown brick, that occupied the center of the complex, designed in a style that might be called interwar Byzantine, and looking pretty much as a part of a church ought to do. Attached to the east and south ends of this struc-ture is a plainer but contemporary wing, which is the church hall, and at the west there is a more recent low, nondescript extension with a short, narrow tower that could be anything. My feeling every time I passed the building was that there is something very sad in the idea that an architect can relate to an ugly suburban area as if it were a corner of a village in Byzantium, just as all those Tudor and "Queen Anne" bank branches and shops of the 1920s are sad because they are in places that could never be transformed into somewhere beautiful. Even if it were possible, it would take many, many decades and similar-minded designers to achieve it, and so even to embark on a project like this is already an admission of a future failure, however much contemporary writers of any period might have talked up the style. You can see something similar every time an architect in Europe or Asia tries to design a building that looks American, or for that matter an American designer tries to build a piece of "Europe" somewhere where it really does not seem to belong.

Much worse, however, is the fact that architectural historians know that there was here, in the immediate vicinity, a terrible architectural loss about fifty years ago, and thus the impressive fact that St. Mark's Church is now the most prominent building in the area is a distinction it simply does not deserve. In a road just behind it sat, until its demolition in the 1960s following war damage and subsequent desuetude, the

FIGURE 4.1
St. Mark's Church, Ramsgate, Kent: the Byzantine chancel (1937) is by Thomas Francis Ford, and its economical nave (1967) by Percy Flaxman. Courtesy of Keith Diplock.

delicate and beautiful Ramsgate municipal airport terminal, a tiny pavilion that looked like the outspread wings of a biplane, captured for a famous photograph of 1937 by Dell & Wainright. The site of this structure to the northeast of the church is now part of an ugly industrial estate, and is occupied by a shed that houses a removals agency and a wine wholesale distributor—no trace whatsoever of the airport remains. Its designer was David Pleydell-Bouverie, an architect who was until 1934 the partner of Wells Coates in London, but who some years afterward left England for California, in the opinion of his obituarist Humphrey Stone a delayed reaction to his cruel upbringing and the bullying of his authoritarian father.[1] On the West Coast he dressed as a cowboy, wore tight jeans, moved into land management, and was married for ten years to Alice Muriel Astor Harding as her fourth husband; the only building he is said to have designed after leaving England was a house for the food writer M. F. K. Fisher.

This much I knew about St. Mark's and the area around it, but initial research revealed a situation that is more disappointing than I had imagined. The "Byzantine" part of the church was designed in the late 1930s by Thomas Francis Ford, at the time an architect for some ten

FIGURE 4.2
Until its demolition in the 1960s, the most significant building in the immediate vicinity of St. Mark's was Ramsgate airport, designed by David Pleydell-Bouverie and captured here by Dell & Wainwright. Dell & Wainwright / RIBA Library Photographs Collection.

years of new churches and alterations to them, and the founder of what has since become a major restoration practice.[2] His short, tall block turns out to be the chancel only of what was intended to be a large and imposing building, for the church's website explains that St. Mark's was to have had a long nave and tower, the completion of which was frustrated by the war. So the western extension—of 1967, by an architect from north London called Percy Flaxman—was an apologetic attempt to complete what was supposed to be a grand building.[3] Flaxman surely intended his little tower to compensate for the lack of the grand 1930s one, just as his "arched" (in fact, straight-sided triangular) concrete lintels were presumably supposed to echo or complement the few more expensive Byzantine arches of what was built of Ford's church.

A lengthy history of the parish that was printed in 1993—the kind of account that records small details from every parish meeting and social event—notes that the original commissioning process was started in 1937 to mark the coronation of King George VI that year but says nothing about the design, or the name of the architect and how he was chosen (a recommendation from the Ecclesiastical Commissioners or diocesan surveyor was the most likely route); it takes no interest in the Byzantine fantasy and fails to record any reaction to it by parishioners.[4] There is no record of Ford's drawings either in the local diocesan collection at Canterbury, or at the Incorporated Church Building Society (ICBS) archive at Lambeth Palace Library, the record center of the Church of England. I then discovered that the vicarage does possess a plan and a perspective view by Ford of a proposal dated May 4, 1937—a week before the king's coronation—and although this appears to be of the final scheme, the Byzantine element is underplayed. In fact the style of the tower, which was to have been at the southwest corner of the long nave, was actually Romanesque, with a timber belfry, so the fragment that was erected gives the wrong impression altogether.[5] Because of the lack of completion, but also because no one among the parishioners is recorded as having found a way of thinking or speaking about it, or recording or publishing their thoughts about it, Ford's dream building will remain a mystery for most. There is slightly more information about Flaxman's extension, perhaps because the author of the parish history remembered its construction from first hand, although the ICBS records, without drawings, only Flaxman's failure to gain an approval, presumably for an earlier scheme, in 1964–1965.[6] There is nothing in the new "Pevsner" guide about the church, although the latest editions generally refer even to small suburban churches, and there is nothing either in the catalog of the British Architectural Library (BAL).

Unlike the story behind Ford's appointment, that of Flaxman's is related in detail in the parish history, evidently because the congregation found this more interesting than the actual design of any building. The vicar in the early 1960s had a brother who was an architect in Edinburgh called Eric Hall, who proposed to design the building without charge; because of the distance involved this was impractical, and the brother asked a colleague of his, who was Flaxman, to carry out the work.[7] Flaxman did this at a reduced fee, and with the assistance of a local architect called David Cox, who died in 2012 and thus cannot be interviewed. The parish history records the following somewhat unenthusiastic observation sometime after the building had been dedicated by the Archbishop of Canterbury in June 1967:

> [Flaxman's] simple and unorthodox building plan effectively fitted the new part to the older, and as time went on it became clearer that there was a great gain in entrusting the whole scheme, including such small but prominent things as the hymnboard, to one mind.[8]

The hymnboard: this is the only architectural reference in the entire history of the hundred years of the parish and its buildings— something of a testament to the gulf between the dreams of architects and their reception by people who cannot understand them. Indeed, the parish history recorded that it was difficult at first to raise interest in the project at all, and thus funds, even for Flaxman's cheap nave.[9]

So the building that has replaced the beautiful, delicate, vulnerable, idealistic butterfly of the Pleydell-Bouverie airport as the major architectural structure of the immediate area is merely this jumble of an unfinished, overambitious building with a cheap extension, the latter of course a victim of its time, a period when to go on building Byzantine or Romanesque would have been unthinkable; Flaxman's little tower is all the more of a disappointing gesture toward Ford's church, because it sits in the same place as the grand one on the unexecuted scheme of May 1937. The first architect's original drawings have disappeared into private ownership: no one had anything to say about them on the record, anyway; and Flaxman's have vanished without trace. There is here no landscaping, or any kind of imposing forecourt. There is no Byzantine village; no picturesque street corner; no colorful realized vision of an exotic *suq*; no Norman village either, no hearty yeomen entering by a stocky bell tower; no happy throng of pious, well-dressed people going gladly about their daily business—just an ugly and largely empty street corner, in the suburb of a small provincial town. I mentioned in my introduction that "disappointment" and "failure" were not metaphors but actual descriptions of loser-buildings: here is one of those, in front of our eyes.

And yet it is here that the real story begins. Although it is possible to work out a conventional description of the church's design and evolution, the evidence suggests that what was built at St. Mark's might be about something else altogether, and that something comes only in fleeting, contradictory, and highly personal fragments. And whereas the conventional narrative will only ever be about a small and unimportant building that will interest almost no one—not even, it appears, the parishioners themselves—the tale behind it is something that touches on the grand themes of life: dreams in a banal world; the frustrations and hopelessness of being an architect; the tragedy of an inconclusive building. And that real tale lies in the relationship of the architects to their buildings.

In Ford's case, his application to become a Fellow of the Royal Institute of British Architects (RIBA) in 1932 was accompanied by a list of his works to date, and in the "publications" section he mentions that he was the author of a thesis on seventeenth-century buildings in the Yorkshire town of Halifax, for which he was awarded a distinction. Ford at least left behind him a flourishing architectural practice that still carries his name; the story of Flaxman, however, demonstrates how easy it is for the records of the life and work of an architect, which are sometimes extensive and revealing, to vanish when there is no documentary evidence of them. The catalog of the BAL has nothing on him, so the buildings he designed himself were not picked up as such by the press and will be hard to identify for future researchers. The RIBA membership department had on record only that he had been a student at the Architectural Association during and after the Second World War, and from this information I found him in retirement at Frinton, on the Essex coast, and spoke to him.[10]

Flaxman's absence from the BAL catalog was explained by the fact that he had spent his career, as an architect and later as a landscape architect, either working for private practices bearing the names of others—mainly, Troup & Steele, the architects known principally for the Brutalist work at King's College, London, and the commercial architects The Ronald Fielding Partnership—or for the government, as a specialist conservation architect for the Directorate of Ancient Monuments and Historic Buildings, a forerunner of today's English Heritage. He had nowhere to store his own collection of architectural drawings when he moved into a smaller home on retirement, so he had destroyed them. I told him that the only Internet reference I had found to him was that he had been employed in mid-1992 as a consultant by Historic Royal Palaces, a government agency, to report on the restoration of the maze in the gardens of Hampton Court Palace.[11] In fact, he then told me, he had been originally called out of retirement to carry out work on the Palace itself, as the restorer of the William III–period apartments there following the fire of 1986; with Pamela Lewis he had refitted out the destroyed rooms with wall hangings and curtains, drawing wherever possible from the original detailed specifications of the late seventeenth century—late Stuart, not quite Queen Anne. While still employed by the Directorate he had worked on the restoration of parts of Kensington Palace in London, another Wren building, converting a derelict, still war-damaged part of the site covered by a temporary roof into the apartments to be used by the newly married Prince and Princess of Wales in 1981; furthermore, he added a William IV–style Doric portico, inspired by the early-nineteenth-century architect and writer W. F. Pocock, to the Palace's north front—a structure invisible to all but Palace residents and their private visitors. There was, Flaxman told me ruefully, very little interest in and money for building in historical styles during the period in which he practiced as a conservation architect. To try to do anything like that, for example for a small church in Ramsgate, would have been intrinsically hopeless.

I found a single reference to Flaxman in print—an article on the design of Danish gardens that he contributed to the *Architectural*

Association Journal in June 1951. This is part of what he had to say about the private garden of Mrs. Erna Friis at Lellinge:

> The iris and soft foliage of the broom will bind the design together as the flowering season moves over the garden and the Hostas take deep shadows and bright reflections under the shade tree. Even the smoothness of the lawn merges into the border—"border" is almost the wrong term to use as it suggests something all too formal—by a transitional planting of the creeping Cotula squallida. . . .
>
> The herbaceous planting is the backbone of this garden, but the wide expanse of lawn and mature feature trees are linked with the long low house by a cloudy froth of lavender, gypsophylla, roses and pink lilies. The drawing room invades the garden here; the roses are all shades of pink and the grey of the lavender is carried over the ground with catmint and prostrate thyme. It is superbly effeminate and the pinks and mauves are blended with the white in a billowing softness.[12]

Deep shadows and bright reflections; the smoothness of the lawn merging into the border; the cloudy froth of lavender and lilies; the billowing softness. An apartment in Kensington for Diana, Princess of Wales, and a new neoclassical porch; tapestries and wall hangings for one of Britain's great palaces. And yet, if the records are anything to go by, all that this architect has to show for himself is a cheap and disappointing 1960s nave dumped unceremoniously on a stretch of mean grass and an asphalted parking lot on a suburban street corner. If Ford's head had once been in the early neoclassical period in Yorkshire, was Flaxman a Regency fantasist, dreaming of Bath, of Beau Brummell, of the Prince Regent at Brighton, sashaying into baroque mazes like the architect in the film *The Draughtsman's Contract*, or flouncing through effeminate Danish gardens as the cities of England still lay in ruins? Had he been working at any period other than the three decades following the Second World War, would he have been able to realize any of the projects he really had a passion for? These are the things that this church is really about, aren't they? These and the departing shadow of David Pleydell-Bouverie, bullied, exiled, finally liberated from a miserable English childhood into tight jeans and Californian sun. It is striking that architects, and especially architecture critics, have a soft spot for fantasy architecture of various types, such as unrealized projects by well-known architects and the architecture of science fiction and adventure films, but almost never show any interest in the fantasies of these everyday architects, which are in many ways at least as interesting and rather touching. What an ordinary suburban failure of a building like St. Mark's tells me above all is that there is likely to be a so-far-unwritten architectural history of some depth and power in every town, a history that can be written in a way that can reach out to people who have difficulties in speaking or writing about buildings. Whether it is about the failed Byzantine or Norman villages, or the fantastic beauty of the Danish garden, and the frustration and hopelessness of trying to realize them on an everyday street corner, there will be something somewhere that means much more to the parishioners of St. Mark's than a set of drawings for a church and its extension.

NO FUTURE

There have also been architects who have been asked to build something with a healthy budget but a long way above their capabilities: an example sometimes given of a building that disappoints by its failure to live up to its site and budget is that of the new house at Eaton Hall in Cheshire, designed for the Duke of Westminster in 1971 by John Dennys, erected on the site of Alfred Waterhouse's superb but unmanageable Gothic mansion which had been demolished eight years earlier except for its chapel and stables.[13] To condemn Dennys, as is often done, as having being chosen because he was the brother-in-law of the duchess is unfair, for he had been a teacher for almost a decade at the Architectural Association during the 1950s, and had recently been president of its council; who knows what else he might have achieved, had not his career and life ended in an accident in Greece in 1973 when he was only 51.[14] Yet his building looked so hopeless, a clumsy blotch in its travertine marble facing, and so pathetic as the termination to a long avenue, that it was later remodeled and refaced in 1989–1991 by the Percy Thomas Partnership, generally known for their commercial and institutional buildings, and now it resembles a stranded, large and provincial, French department store. The real story of the Duke of Westminster's new palace is actually thus the story of its sequences of embarrassment and hopelessness.

Just as there were architects like George Basevi who seemed unable to cope with the demands of the new Gothic Revival, there must have been many more who were defeated by the increased technological demands of architecture from the post-First World War period onward. They sank disappointedly into retrenchment as the expectations for technical expertise demanded of a modern architect folded over their heads, or they became distressed by the way in which architecture seemed now to be about something unfamiliar. The phenomenon must have recurred endlessly right across the Western world. The Danish-Israeli architect Ulrik Plesner recalls in his autobiography that his great-uncle, the distinguished architect of much of the resort town of Skagen on Jutland who bore the same name as himself, discovered that he "suddenly belonged to the past. He died puzzled and sad" in 1933.[15] The fate of Martin Lovell, the architect hero of a novel called *Bricks and Mortar*, written by Helen Ashton and published the year before, seems to reflect that of Plesner, but perhaps more specifically of Basevi himself: born in 1868, he is as a young man enthused by arts and crafts design, the style of his first houses, but as he matures he slowly discovers in himself a growing affinity for Queen Anne and then the Regency. He lives in one of the early-eighteenth-century houses in Barton Street in Westminster, where some of Horace Field's best work, in a romantic version of the same style, would have been visible from his front door. The vulgar Edwardian baroque of the new shops and offices that have replaced Nash's Regent Street disgusts him.[16] At the end of the novel he visits the site of a modernistic building in London designed by his son-in-law Oliver, who has recently returned from New York full of enthusiasm for its jazzy tall buildings. Martin is puzzled by Oliver's building, with its dirty gray concrete frame and its inexplicable proportion of glass to wall; he climbs up the scaffolding, to catch a glimpse of the Wren churches he so enjoyed, and while he is up there, he falls from the ladder to his death. The novel ends immediately. There was, evidently, nowhere left for him to go.

I have mentioned that the striking thing about Quality Street and other hybrid Regency or Georgian revivals is that those who promoted them already knew that historically these were doomed styles; and we know now that the people who enjoyed them most in the 1920s and 1930s were aesthetes. They remembered that the Gothic Revival had finished off this whimsical, lightweight neoclassical architecture, so well suited, in their own times, to tea rooms and Bond Street shoe shops: in fact one clear achievement of the Quality Street style is that it actually could bring a touch of Bond Street to every town center parade. Is there, I wonder, a death wish involved with this revival, a pushing of one's own head under the waves? One of Field's least effective projects was to try to give an elegant Regency face to the austere, aggressive Gothic of Edward Pugin's Granville Hotel in Ramsgate. He added a veranda topped by a little white timber pediment to the front, decorated with his characteristic bold dentils; he affixed Quality Street-style wrought-iron railings to the façades; and he reduced the height of the building's monstrous tower, shaving off the outer planes of its projecting oriel windows which ever since have looked like the victims of a botched medical intervention. In the perspective of his scheme that was published in the *Architect* on November 2, 1900, the remodeled building is depicted as a cheerful place, with plenty of greenery

FIGURE 4.3
Horace Field's additions and alterations to Edward Pugin's Granville Hotel, Ramsgate, in 1900 included the addition of a Quality Street veranda in white timber and the mutilation of its tower. Courtesy of Keith Diplock.

writhing around its many balconies in an unconvincing attempt to smother some of its ineradicable Gothicness. But the jolly bandstand and the contented holiday crowds fool nobody. It was a hopeless assignment; it could not have been done well by anyone.

Now Edward Pugin is famous again, and Field is not, so Field clocks up a further failure as the mutilator of a "better" building by somebody else. But Field at least was a good designer at the time. Being a second- or third-rate architect, and having as part of your record the mutilation of a fine building by someone better, is a true hallmark of loserdom. The website of Pembroke College, Cambridge, records the names of some of the great designers who contributed to its architecture: Wren (the college chapel in its original form was his first completed work); Alfred Waterhouse; George Gilbert Scott junior; W. D. Caröe; Eric Parry.[17] The list does not include Maurice Webb, the eldest and not particularly talented son of the successful and well-regarded architect Aston Webb, in the late Victorian and Edwardian era the designer of significant London monuments such as the main block of the Victoria and Albert Museum, and the processional route from Trafalgar Square to Buckingham Palace, including the Victoria Monument and the front face of the palace itself. Webb junior, who took over the running of his father's practice in the early 1920s, was a graduate of Pembroke. He mutilated Waterhouse's high-Gothic dining hall in 1926 by lowering the ceiling and adding fatuous, uncomfortable, Quality Street features; and in 1933 he designed a new master's lodge in the style of a characterless, flat-faced dolls' house where I once was refused admission to join my parents for lunch by the then master, a building which anyhow has now vanished under a much-praised building by Parry.

Webb has other strong claims to hopelessness. He died aged only 59, just before the Second World War; and traces of him are being eradicated from other places too. His most successful building was a department store (1931–1935) called Bentalls in Kingston upon Thames, just outside London; it was designed in a version of Wren's Hampton Court style, something of an optimistic gesture given that the proximity of Webb's store to the real thing makes an unflattering comparison easily achievable. Bentalls was gutted in stages between 1987 and 1992 for a new shopping center; a publication called *The*

Bentall Centre Fact File, put out by the developers, credits the old building not to Maurice Webb but to his more famous father, just as plenty of dull buildings by Peter Paul Pugin are still often credited by their residents to his father Augustus.[18] Furthermore, anyone visiting Kingston today will soon have their attention drawn by the much-admired branch of the John Lewis department store chain, designed in 1979 by Ahrends, Burton and Koralek, which, unfortunately for Webb's reputation, is located opposite the remaining skin of his "Hampton Court" elevation: what critic will turn the other way with anything but contempt for poor Webb, even in the unlikely event that they have ever heard of him? The *London: North West* "Pevsner" condemns Webb's other major structure, the 1929 Beit Building, in South Kensington for Imperial College, also inaccurately attributed online (by the college itself) to his father, as being in "the terrible style of the reactionaries of the 1920s"; and in *London South* the same authors say of Webb's Kingston Guildhall that its peculiar curved entrance façade is "not a balanced or well composed front."[19] Thus little of Maurice Webb's reputation will survive unless some brave soul from the

FIGURE 4.4
The surviving façade of Maurice Webb's Bentalls department store, Kingston upon Thames, Surrey: unfortunately it can easily be compared with the real baroque of Christopher Wren's Hampton Court Palace nearby. Courtesy of Keith Diplock.

Twentieth Century Society decides to rehabilitate him for the pleasure of the tiny number of enthusiasts who follow the careers of the cursed and the hopeless. Perhaps only his Quality Street-style north elevation to Robert Adam's Royal Society of Arts, toward the Strand in London, will save him from oblivion.

FIGHTING THE WALLS

Much of interior design is inherently hopeless too, in this case in the sense that the results are unresolved or unresolvable, in the way that an architect generally tries to resolve the overall design of a building. One can see this as a battle between a designer brought in later, or without having been consulted on the structure and layout, and the hard concrete facts of the walls that have been put there by someone else, someone whose access to high-art criticism is always going to be easier than theirs. In any case, interior design is temporary, and meant to be temporary, whereas until recently architects believed—as Ruskin told them to—that they, by contrast, were building forever. And yet here I can see how much architectural criticism can learn from studying it. The sadnesses of it are more immediate than those of architecture, and anyone can spot them right away. I am looking at the moment at a recent book of photographs of British domestic interiors and I am struck—in spite of their attractiveness, which is real—by how sad they are. Houses that are too tidy for real life, too mannered; rooms inhabited, if that is the right word, by childless male couples and by assertive businesswomen, or so it appears from the small amount of explanatory text provided; here are rare and beautiful musical instruments that are, one supposes, little played; here are piles of magazines that are moved for different shots, for the sake of the camera; here are vases of flowers—the latter reminding me, unfairly, of the comment anecdotally attributed to the French interior designer Madeleine Castaing that wilting cut flowers are like dead bodies. There is much evidence here of the calculated self-image, much easier and cheaper to achieve through interior design than through a real building, many people still trusting the comment by P. A. Barron, writing between the two world wars, that "owners of charming houses are always charming people," a declaration that is somehow unlikely to be true.[20] If you live on your own, or if you do not have a family, you might well invest all your efforts in this paper-thin, transient thing that will die when you die, or beforehand: you will bequeath it to your favorite nephew, who will most likely put nearly all of it out in the skip.

The fakeness, the unreality, the slightly mystic quality attributed to inanimate things, the setting up of a façade against a largely artless and ugly world like putting on bold, inappropriate makeup—the whole enterprise has an antiestablishment feel to it, as had the oceans of pious gaudy junk that used to occupy Catholic churches in Protestant England. It is again the architecture of defiance. None of these things is "real" in the way architects defined the word: they are expressions of protest founded on a whole armory of wishful thinking. For surely these "charming" people are trying to put right, through the design of their houses, the one thing in their life that they can control, something that was not right for them in the past; just as there are people who spend time imagining a reconciliation to put right any kind of personal relationship that ended badly, trying to make the nasty person nice in their own minds, single-handedly, unable of course to do any such thing in reality.

The result can be a series of interiors within a single house that do not lie neatly with one another, or speak the same language as one another, in the way that the architecture of rooms within a building nearly always does. None of this is meant to suggest that the designers of domestic interiors are charlatans; far from it. There is no doubting the power of what an interior is like; I remember going back to the house I grew up in and seeing how my mother's pretty decoration scheme had been replaced by horrible, artless colors: it caused me something of a real and lasting trauma. What I am saying is that interior design can shed a light on the hopeless aspect of architecture, the wanting something to be what it is not, with a limited budget, a narrow and fussy vision of completeness, and an avoidance of dealing with the big, expensive things. My picture book of romantic interiors projects a comprehensive image of the tremendous futility of what is, in purely architectural terms, a wasted effort, an attempt to create or re-create a beautiful life through the thin dimension only of walls and cushions. Maybe that is why I like it, for I also like the washed-out views of

Edwardian and interwar interiors in the many books I collect on the subject: they are a further expression of my own hopelessness. I don't need to read the accompanying text, which is anyway only rarely illuminating; just glimpsing the old photographs is enough to do the job.

I mentioned just now that there can be a battle between interior designers and architects, and twenty-five years ago I experienced this at first hand. A professional interior designer stripped out the interior (without permission) of an apartment in a smart part of London, revealed the underside of a sunken bath projecting from the floor above, panicked, and finally called in some architects—us—to sort it out. When pictures of the flat were subsequently published in a well-known interiors magazine, the involvement of architects in the project was completely ignored: she told the world that she had done it on her own. This episode illustrates to me something of the gulf between two professions that have less in common with one another than is generally thought by laymen. One of the things I was struck by when working myself in an architectural practice that specialized in remodeling the interiors of Victorian houses in London was that non-architects are so scared of moving staircases and doors—in reality no great problem or expense—that they will move everything else about in their idea of a plan in order to leave them where they are. This in itself expresses something further about the detached nature of interior design compared to architecture.

Here I am becoming a bully myself, of course, because of the suggestion, as an architect or architecture critic, that the only thing that matters is the fabric of the building itself and the things that the original architect thought should be affixed to it. We know that eighteenth-century architects working on high-prestige projects saw the design of the interior as being part of the house; in the past when I have claimed that Pugin was the first to design a coherent set of architectural details for both inside and out, I have been reminded by those with a more balanced view of history that Robert Adam, and top-end Georgian architects working on prestige projects, also did this. But it was Pugin who made it important to architects to maintain this coherence. He had achieved it in his domestic architecture by the time he finished his own house in Ramsgate in 1844, and from exactly then onward he went on to realize it on a spectacular scale at the Palace of Westminster: "You

may search the Houses of Parliament from top to bottom," wrote
Voysey ecstatically in 1915, "and you will not find one superficial yard
that is copied from any pre-existing building"—and there are, of
course, many thousands of details there.[21] The same complete control
of the interior, exactly corresponding to and relating to the details of
the exterior, is characteristic of the work of Pugin's admirers fifty years
later—Voysey and others—to the extent that by the turn of the twentieth century, so perfect is the fit between the details and the exact use
and character of a room that each place in a house can be used by the
resident only in precisely the way that the architect originally intended.
The international influence of the British arts and crafts movement
brought with it the common acceptance among designers that this
should be the case, eventually creating what Hermann Muthesius went
on to call "the emotion-laden furniture" that made these buildings
impossibly stifling.[22] At much the same time Adolf Loos coined the
expression "Poor Little Rich Man" to satirize the way in which rich
clients found themselves at the mercy of their architect's *Gesamtkunst-
werk* interior, to the extent that they had no freedom any more in what
they could do, or even think, within their own houses.[23]

The high-art international modern movement was the third
attempt at forcing on the general public the notion that architecture
and interior design are indivisible. And yet they are not, which is why
they keep coming apart in the great majority of buildings that are completed beneath the critical radar. As David Watkin wrote in his *Radical
Classicism: The Architecture of Quinlan Terry*, responding to criticism,
mainly in the *Architectural Review*, of the apparent conflict between the
crafted neo-Georgian exteriors and the unremarkable modern office
interiors of Terry's Richmond Riverside scheme:

> in the needless pursuit of the doctrine of "truth" in the religion of
> Modernist architecture, it has been insisted that interior and exte-
> rior should always be one and the same thing. However the com-
> plex story of architecture teaches us a very different lesson.[24]

It was in reaction to the stifling nature of arts and crafts design that
architects turned back to the simplicity and versatility of Georgian-type
rooms, where you could put your furniture and yourself where you

pleased and when you felt like it. The interior designers of this period were doing exactly what the unremembered Edwardian architects in chapter 2 were doing: they were creating, with the help of furniture shop decorators, a variety of styles and atmospheres under the same roof. This was also the period when there was a flowering of fine illustrated children's books. I wonder whether some of those images might themselves be a reflection of the hopelessness of the interior designer, a retreat into infantilization when faced with the reality of adulthood. The whole enterprise of interior design has about it all the hallmarks of an inherently tragic endeavor.

SETTING THE RULES

Although coherence between rooms is less important for interior designers and their clients, the creation of a total environment, preferably a fantastic one of some sort, is much valued. The great achievement of Castaing is derived from the fact that her rooms were made up from a dense and eclectic mixture of pieces—including, after the Second World War, the English Regency—so their power lay in her layering of historical associations; the confused sense of completeness that they evidently projected elicited associations and references from several conflicting sources at once. Basil Ionides, a quite different designer from the interwar period, also aimed to create complete environments, but using other means. His 1926 book *Colour and Interior Decoration* provides charts that tell the amateur decorator what colors and materials should be used in details as small as the fringes of curtains or lampshades, and the mounts of pictures, giving the lie, to anyone who thought otherwise, to the idea that only architects and perhaps set or theater designers are interested in total control. The book has the commanding nature that one would expect from a designer who grew up in Kensington in a family circle rooted in collecting and in the aesthetic movement—his father Luke was a friend of J. M. Whistler, and his uncle and aunt were both patrons and friends of William Morris and the pre-Raphaelite artists. Basil Ionides worked in upper-class circles, was friendly with the aristocratic designers Syrie Maugham and Mrs. Guy Bethell (he illustrated her work in

DECORATIVE SCHEMES IN BLUE.

Walls.	Woodwork.	Ceiling.	Floor.	Curtains.	Covers.	Cushions.	Ornaments.
For a Blue Dining-Room: Painted pale blue and stippled with a blue-black glaze, matte finish. Venetian glass mirrors and cut glass wall lights.	Same as walls, but glossy in surface.	Glossy white.	Dark blue, varnished. Blue and white modern Chinese carpet.	Blue damask with silver-grey fringe of artificial silk. Next to glass, grey artificial silk, edged with apple-green ribbon.	Blue moiré with braid of grey silk at edges. Small chairs, blue diaper damask, edged with grey silk braid.	Blue shantung silk, with narrow frills of same material around the edges.	Nankin blue china; copper or steel. Lampshades lined pink, on cut glass fittings.
For a Town Study or Sitting-Room: Distempered a deep Wedgwood blue. *Pictures:* Old mezzotints.	Painted same colour as walls but slightly darker; matte surface.	Parchment colour, matte surface.	Black, with mauve Samarkand rugs.	Cretonne, Chinese pattern of birds and foliage on blue ground; lined with pink. Next to glass, gold artificial silk, edged with fringe that picks up the colours in main curtains.	Same as curtains for settee, etc. Small chairs of blue velveteen, edged with the fringe that decorates the window curtains.	Taffeta in orange and yellow edged with the curtain fringe.	Copper; pink lustre; Chinese blue vases. Lampshades, orange of Oriental figures and vases.
For a Panelled Room: Flat surfaces painted light blue (mixture of Prussian blue and white); mouldings painted one coat light indigo; the whole stippled with indigo. *Pictures:* Oil paintings in gold frames.	Same as walls.	Very pale blue wash.	Painted indigo and varnished. Carpet, blue Indian imitation of Persian.	Dove-grey damask with bright blue fringe, and lined with very pale pink. Next to glass, pale pink artificial silk with silver galon border.	Blue ground chintz with pattern of large roses in colours, lined with pale green. Small chairs, blue trellis chintz, edged with gold galon.	Several shades of pink edged with gold galon.	Brass; copper; blue and white china. Lampshades, pink silk on stands of gilded wood.
For a Country Cottage Room: Pale pastel blue wash. Woolwork pictures of ships.	Bleached pale grey with oxalic acid, then given one coat of whitewash, wiped off, leaving white in grain.	White.	Pale grey bleached with oxalic acid and scrubbed. Rush matting.	Pale blue shantung silk, unlined, with fringe at bottom. Next to glass, white book muslin.	Blue cloth, the colour of French uniforms. Small chairs the same, but a different blue, and edged with silver galon.	Grey pale alpaca, edged with blue braid.	Brass; blue and white peasant pottery. Introduce a few notes of orange. Lampshades, white silk lined with yellow, with blue binding, on lamps made of earthenware jars.

FIGURE 4.5

A table from Basil Ionides' *Colour and Interior Decoration* (1926) which describes how precisely to achieve a desired effect.

Colour and Interior Decoration), and designed short-lived interiors for Claridges and the Savoy, the smart London hotels.

No doubt a powerful attraction in the work of both Castaing (mess, eclecticism) and Ionides (order, coherence), which on the face of it seem quite distinct, is the fact that the clients of interior designers seem to have a particular fear of one small element being out of place, one feature which will in some way betray their anxieties about their social status or personal taste. Ionides' two books certainly project a minefield for the insecure, because in his opinion making a mistake in the precise hue of a color can put the decorator in danger of committing the most terrible social *faux pas*: "A bright pink carpet is an abomination, but a crushed strawberry or old rose one may be effective. . . . Pink and gold are apt to cloy, but a little gold with pink is effective. . . . Pink and blue is flowery in its effect, but the blue must be light in tone and should be on the warm purple side . . ." are typical examples from a single page of *Colour and Interior Decoration*.[25] This seems to go some way beyond an architect's fear that a detail has not been resolved satisfactorily, which is a matter not of class or taste but simply of coherence and logic. I remember one client of ours, remodeling a large house in South Kensington, who was worried about the height of light switches. He had them moved up the wall and then, after thinking and worrying, back down again—his fear was that they would shame him, either from being too high, and thus low-class, or, worse, from being too low to avoid being too high, forcing him to commit a lower-middle-class genteelism as bad as saying "toilet" for lavatory. The design of non-Victorian items such as shower cubicles also distressed him, because there was no established high-class precedent. The nitpicking by upper-middle-class viewers of supposedly solecistic details spotted in the internationally successful TV drama *Downton Abbey* shows how perpetually fascinating these things are for the British.[26] If you are an interior designer associated with the wrong class of person, then you are cast into outer darkness as far as the class which sees itself as superior is concerned. This is not generally true of architecture, which has written into its history and consciousness the importance of being able to deal with cheap and simple houses, and where the significance of social class lies only in budgets.

Looking at the practice of interior design thus not only illustrates the hopeless side of architecture, it also greatly increases the scope of that hopelessness, which in turn gives critics much more to think and write about. It more usually projects fantastic rooms, divorced from the reality of the space they occupy, reinforced by unimportant but strict rules, a device usually seen as the refuge of the administrator rather than of the creative artist; it is transient; it evades real problems; it cannot create space, merely divide it up with small pieces; its literature is narrow, and similarly divided into small areas. It tries to create a completeness that is distinct from the physical nature of building and is more closely linked with the ideal world of an individual—which in turn means that, unlike nearly all architecture, a single person can shape and control it. It is possible, of course, to tell the story of its development over time, but this does not evolve in the way that architectural history does; it therefore has no real narrative behind it beyond a reflection on a series of trends in consumerism and social aspiration. All of these things suggest approaches that ought to be useful to architecture critics. The fact that interior design is of so broad an interest to so many people, as witnessed by the array of magazines about it addressed to different audiences, suggests that an appreciation of it is much broader than appreciation of architecture. And therefore, in spite of its lack of substance, it seems to project something which most writing about architecture lacks. The difference between interior design and the design of whole towns, which I shall look at in conclusion, is not much more than a matter of degree; but once one deploys the apprehensions involved in the design of the spare bedroom, or the private sitting room, at the scale of the city, one starts to be confronted with an image of desperate inadequacy.

> I will do such things,—

says the decorator with the roll of wallpaper upstairs,

> What they are, yet I know not: but they shall be
> The terrors of the earth.[27]

HISTORICAL HOPELESSNESS AND WHAT IT IS HIDING

Just as some elements of the great works of John Vanbrugh end up on the front elevations of public housing, so aspects of the creations of the famous practitioners of interior design find themselves recommended for modest suburban dwellings. I have a copy of a book called *The House Improved*, written by Randal Phillips, a prolific author on the subject of modern homes and what to do with them, published by *Country Life* in 1931: it is a book that tells aspiring homemakers how, having given up any hope of commissioning a new house in the postwar economic climate, they can convert an existing one into a comfortable modern residence. The book shows its readers how to enter into a hopeless battle with Victorian architecture: how to demolish, or mutilate, or alter it out of existence so that it becomes streamlined, pastel-colored, modern. There were many books of this kind which emerged together with the development of the interior designer as a person distinct from a representative of a furniture shop, marking again the point at which interior design once more becomes divorced from architectural criticism, as it had been in the days when each room in a large Victorian house might have been designed in a different style. This is one which suggests a number of battle lines between the exterior and interiors of the buildings. But more interesting for me is the fact that once one looks into the projects carefully, and follows up their subsequent lives, one discovers that the book is full of architectural tragedies in different senses: some violent, some pathetic.

Phillips's book opens with a view of a pair of houses in Palace Street, close to Buckingham Palace; the right-hand one is a Georgian terraced cottage, with ugly, narrow, two-paned sash windows and no ornament at all except for the fact that there is a semicircular brick fanlight; the house to the left has been turned into Quality Street by forcing onto its fabric genteel decoration and details: the windows have become "Queen Anne," employing the type of timber window construction with prominent sash cord boxes that was outlawed in 1707 as a measure against fire spread; there is a Regency-era bow window; and there is a doorcase from anywhere in the eighteenth century, a perfect hybrid very soon imitated, as it happens, by all the other house-owners in the terrace.[28]

Converting a workers' terrace close to Buckingham Palace into Quality Street was a perfectly reasonable endeavor, but few of Phillips's readers would have been able to manage it; to them are dedicated the sections that follow, explaining how to camouflage an ornamental Victorian marble fireplace into a modern one with some boxing in; ornamental balusters, likewise, with more boxing in; the application of wallboard, a cheap and nasty material, in order to arrive at a stream-lined contemporary interior; how to apply white stucco and French-looking shutters to an ugly house to make it look pretty.[29] The strangest project of the book is the conversion—by Percy Morley Horder, later a successful commercial and institutional architect—of the St. John's

FIGURE 4.6
Before and after: an attempt at converting the front of a plain Victorian terraced house
into a stylish modern façade, from Randal Phillips's *The House Improved.*

Wood house of Lawrence Weaver, *Country Life*'s most distinguished
architectural writer of the period.[30] Here Morley Horder removed the
raised ground-floor entrance that is so characteristic of the large mid-
Victorian detached townhouses of the period and brought visitors in
through the basement, creating a peculiar unbalanced effect on the
street façade as part of his assault on the traditional layout of the
kitchen offices. It is hardly surprising that a subsequent remodeling has
returned the front door to the upper ground floor, taking with it, as an
interesting architectural relic, Weaver's fanlight, now the only detail in
the house that has survived from his period as well as being the only
trace of the Horder project that recalls his short-lived and thus failed
intervention.

    Other projects in the book have considerable charm, yet they too,
as it turns out, may be concealing tragedies: there is a Mayfair stable
behind Park Lane converted solecistically (twice over) into a rural cottage, now demolished; and a Kensington studio in Aubrey Walk made
into a rustic retreat—with prominent ceiling joists—for the disappointed widow of the editor of *Boys of the Empire*, "A magazine for

British Boys all over the world," the aim of which was "To promote and strengthen a worthy imperial spirit in British-born boys."[31] Lady Handley Spicer, who commissioned the conversion, might have been in need of modest and small-scale accommodation because her husband, whom she had sued for restitution of conjugal rights, had recently committed suicide. Of course none of this desperately sad and personal information was mentioned by Phillips, but its discovery certainly shows how a little digging (even, I confess, in this case from Wikipedia) can start to tell the parts of the story that an architecture critic might miss or find irrelevant.[32]

Spicer's tiny house was converted by Arthur T. Bolton, curator of Sir John Soane's Museum at the time; like Bolton's other buildings, it rewards some close attention.[33] The house he designed for himself in Birchington on the north Kent coast—immortalized in his well-known *Small Country Houses of Today* by none other than Lawrence Weaver, whom we have just met—has been horribly enlarged and mutilated in modern times.[34] The world of small house building in any country is not so large that it is impossible to map out the links between the various people and the sites, and from these we get a much broader picture of architectural history, one with links to the culture and society of a particular time. And in turn, an interesting story of some sort will inevitably emerge.

Striking contrasts, or architectural solecisms and anachronisms expressed in the interior and the exterior of buildings, are by no means a sign of tragedy. Although high-art architecture in all its forms generally retained the integration between the interior design and the exterior whatever the style, architects sometimes created an exaggerated contrast between a formal interior and an informal exterior: Edwin Lutyens himself did this in 1908–1909 at Whalton Manor in Northumberland, where he placed a grand staircase and set of rooms, including a circular drawing room, behind the little-altered façade of a row of old cottages. Field also did it, on a smaller scale—from my copy of W. Shaw Sparrow's *Flats, Urban Houses and Cottage Homes* one can see that the plain rendered Edwardian-Tudor-vernacular of the exterior of a house called Hookerel, close to Field's own home by Woking golf course in Surrey, nicely conceals a white-painted, formal classical staircase and interiors; and Field's more successful contemporary E. Guy Dawber installed grand, overscaled but authentically Queen Anne-style ornamental plaster ceilings to low rooms in his redbrick, red-tiled vernacular-style cottage in Berkshire.[35] In all these cases, the contrast was intentional, designed to create an artful paradox: the coherence of the overall design lay in precisely that contrast. It is a shame that architects do not seem able to attempt this nowadays, and when circumstances demand it—as in the case of Terry's Richmond scheme or his (in this respect) comparable Margaret Thatcher Infirmary of 2005–2008 at the Royal Hospital, Chelsea—the result seems to be apology or embarrassment rather than proud resolution.[36]

In any case, most people did not see the architect's prized qualities of coherence and integration as important, and still do not. As architectural magazines turned modernist in the mid-1930s—as we saw happen to the *Architects' Journal*—the advertisements in those same magazines, and the interior design press, remained resolutely eclectic. It is hardly surprising that the modern profession of interior designer emerges as the idea wanes, among those who could afford it, that the person who does the inside of a house must necessarily be the person who does the outside. Maybe the reason for this is the one that Phillips identified—that the building of a new house may be impossible, so one has to make the best of an unsatisfactory or indeed hopeless or almost hopeless situation; maybe another reason was the terrific range of potential interiors that designers across the whole range of the market were then offering: Regency; Tudor; "Queen Anne," generally available through the furnishing departments of the large stores. We saw that Eltham Palace, like many other top-end rich people's houses of the period, had interiors in different styles; only the minor ones were devised by Seely and Paget themselves, and even then not very remarkably. This seems to be what people want, if they can afford it, and to my mind there is nothing wrong with it.

There is no suggestion either that all interior design is attempting to realize the same thing, any more than all architecture is attempting the same thing; in fact the vast number of interior design magazines currently available in the United States and Britain, not to mention elsewhere, gives a good impression of the range available. A fact that is possibly not appreciated consciously by the readers of these magazines is that each one aims at a readership with a different but identifiable set

of priorities; the range from Condé Nast, for example, is easily definable. *House & Garden* illustrates the kind of interiors that anyone can
achieve with almost any building providing they have the money; by
contrast, *The World of Interiors*, to which I have contributed for nearly
twenty-five years, presents interiors that are not achievable by the average reader because they rely, for their impact, on historical situations,
or very unusual architectural circumstances, or a degree of idiosyncratic
creativity. In each case this is precisely what attracts readers to buy a
copy. If you look through what is on offer at even only a medium-sized
newsagent's, you can identify the different parts of the market: there
are, for example, magazines aimed at those who want to achieve a
"green" interior, or a historical one, or a historical one on a low budget,
or something they can make themselves. In each case there is usually
also an impressive degree of editorial consistency. I recommend to
aspiring writers hoping to freelance in this market that they buy the
whole lot, and decide which one speaks to them directly: there are so
many available that they are bound to find something. Then all they
have to do is to imitate the style of writing of that publication, and they
may well quickly be adopted as a contributor.

This variety of writing, some of it based on only very little actual
information, all contributes to a wider understanding of what interior
design is about; architectural writing does not have anything like this
range. The only type of writing on interior design that I find incomprehensible is that found in the interiors supplements of the regular
daily broadsheet newspapers: these generally praise places the attraction of which is to me entirely hidden. Sometimes they are written by
the real-estate correspondents who pride themselves, I suspect, on total
detachment from the whims of architects, whose names they sometimes even omit from the article. The newspapers' editors seem to
believe (and they are surely right) that the real-estate approach to interior design has a readership much larger than that of architectural criticism. In this respect there is a certain parallel between this and popular
archaeology, which—inexplicably to me and to greater people than me,
such as David Watkin—is enormously popular and politically strong:
perhaps it is because most people see things in simple concrete terms,
and cannot cope with bigger and more conceptual ideas.[37] Perhaps also
some people like to see their world defined in small, quantifiable items

that they can control. The battle lines between the different types of writing on interior design can be as fascinating as those between the different types of architecture, and they can draw more people into a circle of debate. But a battle it is, which means that, like every other branch of architecture, it has not only winners and losers, but also stages of retrenchment and, finally, of loss.

RETRENCHMENT AND LOSS

ENDLESS LOSS

In the end, nothing will prevent an original, imaginative, finely thought out, and well-crafted building from being more interesting to architects than any number of structures that fail in those respects, however much we may find to say about both them and the places they came from. No amount of words will compensate for something that is second-rate in the conventional architectural sense—indeed, that was precisely the tragedy that I started out by describing. But this is as much as anything a book about how architecture is communicated through words. A charming or funny or clever, or merely well-disciplined and plain build-ing has a lot to say to us and for us to pass on, and sometimes so does an ugly or unsuccessful one. What we have discovered is that the aspect of architecture most usually underrated in conventional architectural narratives is that of the architect's own relationship with, and experi-ence of, the design and construction of their buildings as objects that are a significant part of their lives, and it would help if critics, at least, made more use of their personal experience, no matter what aspect of it, when they came to try to write about them. Doing so may suggest how to make a story out of what looks like a very ordinary building, and how to link different aspects of the architects' aspirations and achievements in a way that communicates the value of architecture to others. After all, in some cases architecture is born out of desperate feelings, feelings that go as deep as any others in life, and more often than not this des-peration is born out of a downward trajectory, a recognition that

something is not right—the unrewarded desperation captured by Philip
Larkin in his poem "Faith Healing":

> An immense slackening ache
> As when, thawing, the rigid landscape weeps,
> Spreads slowly through them

Much of this book has concentrated on the desperations of the
1920s and 1930s, the period described by the historian Richard Overy
as the "morbid" one. There is evidence that the increasingly ugly subur-
banization of the English countryside was then causing distress to aes-
thetically sensitive people. A book of 1929 by P. A. Barron, the writer
who thought that charming people lived in charming houses and who
enthusiastically promoted the building of Tudor-style homes, is typical:

> Everywhere, we see new houses which can only be described as
> hideous. Everywhere, our once beautiful country is being disfig-
> ured, and estates are being cut up into tiny plots upon which are
> erected modern villas and bungalows which are ill proportioned,
> often badly built, and so ugly that strangers might suppose us to be
> a nation of barbarians totally lacking a sense of beauty.[1]

Only recently his highbrow equivalent, Clough Williams-Ellis,
had published a polemic called *England and the Octopus* which made a
similar and broader point, if more delicately:

> Everyone who reads this book—indeed everyone who reads at all
> or has eyes in his head—knows that England has changed violently
> and enormously in the last few decades. Since the War, indeed, it
> has been changing with an acceleration that is catastrophic, thor-
> oughly frightening the thoughtful among us, and making them
> sadly wonder whether anything recognisable of our lovely England
> will be left for our children's children.[2]

Nothing is left. Endless loss. It was an exaggeration, of course.
These are people who had seen the Great War; who had no doubt lost
family and friends; who had perhaps been traumatized; who now saw

war memorials, some in the form of images of idealized or even naked, vulnerable young soldiers, going up around them. And now the cherished landscape of rural England was collapsing around them too: a strange, distressing combination of feelings and images. Sometimes life is so terrible that you have a feeling inside you that all you want to do is to chuck out everything you know and start from scratch; only very rarely in someone's life is it possible to make this happen in reality. In particular, there are architects who have tried to make a whole new world—or the closest thing to it—in order to escape from a reality they do not like. It is the redecorating of the upstairs bedroom on a grand scale. This is not an isolated historical occurrence: it is a phenomenon which can happen at any time.

This was, after all, essentially the aim of the American New Urbanism movement, which reached its most influential stage in the early 1990s, and was captured in a book of 1994, by Peter Katz, called *The New Urbanism: Toward an Architecture of Community*. This was a dream cult that happened to realize some buildings. For the fascinating thing about the manifestos of the movement—as they were described by, for example, Peter Calthorpe, Andrés Duany, and Elizabeth Plater-Zyberk in essays in Katz's book—is that their principles of planning were not really substantially different to those seen in the public sector across Europe in general and Britain in particular since the war. The stated aims of the New Urbanists included planning based on walking distances within distinct neighborhoods; some minor level of mixed use in residential areas; and distinct pedestrian, cycle, and vehicular corridors: all of these came virtually unchanged out of Ebenezer Howard's Garden City movement, and had gone on to form the basis for the type of public-sector housing that went up in Britain in the 1950s and 1960s until rising land costs and experiments in economic large-scale systems building, and a fashion for Brutalism, brought it to an end.

In postwar Britain the imagery deployed by planners was profoundly romantic: it was that of the low-density Swedish suburb as it had been published in the *Architectural Review*, and books on Scandinavian planning and architecture during the Second World War and the years that followed. What architects then saw—as they sat hungry and tired in a military encampment, or bored and nervous in a London house in a ravaged street, half bombed or full of rats—was a carefully

FIGURE 5.1
The ideal city vision of the New Urbanists: a perspective view of canal
villas from a project for an unbuilt town in Florida, by DPZ & Company
(Charles Barrett and Manuel Fernandez-Noval, artists), 1989. © DPZ
(Charles Barrett & Manuel Fernandez-Noval, artists).

edited selection of images from the most picturesque of the Stockholm
suburbs—Ekhagen, Traneberg, Danviken, Gröndal: to me poetic,
wonderful names. This was what was in their heads when they went on
to design the New Towns of the late 1940s onward and the first postwar public housing: a sentimental, picturesque image, with connotations too of an agreeable and appealing political system; and so it was
exactly to be with the New Urbanists reacting to the ugliness of modern
speculative building. The only real difference between the two types is
the visual image of the town that the New Urbanists projected, and the
degree of control they wanted over it: in Katz's book there are Lutyens-
like town centers and blatant bits of New Englandery; and there are
Tuscan villas set amid rivers and lush northern greenery for a site in
Florida. And from Katz's book I discovered that Duany and Plater-
Zyberk's design codes "are the most elaborate and tightly drawn—
sometimes dictating the thickness of mortar between bricks."[3] So
American New Urbanism—the kind where every aspect of a plan,
including the activities and behaviors in it, is prescribed by its designers—is specifically derived from the English arts and crafts view that all
of life could be reformed on artistic principles providing that there was

logic and order to it, even if doing so flew in the face of economic reality. All that had really happened since the 1920s was that planning had become institutionalized—which meant that large public authorities had begun to supplant private or local ones—and the car had begun to dominate planning. To give a further example of the similarity between the New Urbanists and the early-twentieth-century pioneers: one ambition of Katz's protagonists is that building permissions can be given quickly, because the overall town plan is so detailed that little choice is left to an individual private house-builder. This was precisely the aim of the British Mandate-imposed planning system, devised by that noble failure Charles Ashbee, that has survived in Israel and Jordan, made simple there by the fact that nearly all land was owned by the state. The contributors to Katz's book admit their origins: his preface notes that the source of New Urbanism lies in "the years 1900–1920 (now coming to be regarded as a watershed era in the history of urban design)."[4] For New Urbanism was a matter of taste, that is all, not of principle; it was simply a new expression of the familiar defiance in the face of the disappointments of the modern city. Indeed, the planning ideas of the New Urbanists were, ironically, often precisely the same ones that had produced the type of loose, often characterless urban spaces that they themselves disliked.

FIGURE 5.2
The British Scandinavianists designed townscapes at least as romantic as those of the New Urbanists: this is Twydall, north Kent, from the early 1960s. Courtesy of Keith Diplock.

As is often the case with architecture, then, the talk is not about the reality. It is significant that a caption to the chapter by Todd W. Bressi in Katz's book states that Duany and Plater-Zyberk's practice "relies on carefully drawn and colored renderings to convey a romantic, historicist impression of its proposals."[5] So in this case there was romance not simply in the design idea, but also in the drawings, which were invested with some power independent of their role as blueprints for approval or construction purposes. There seems to be an acceptance that their fantasy imagery is mainly unrealizable on the scale they require to do what they are supposed to do. To have books on New Urbanism, to drink in the pleasures of the idealized perspectives in them and yet to know that they are unrealized and unrealizable, and to be unable to do anything about it—all this is, I think, profoundly sad.

In Britain it was possible to implement a great deal of this romantic-fantasy Swedish-style planning because it had the arm of the newly empowered public planning authorities behind it; by contrast the New Urbanism, in spite of the noise made at the time, has remained largely dreamlike and fantastical. Not much has materialized nearly twenty years on from the schemes that Katz illustrated relative to the interest they generated; some plans evidently never got off the ground, and few have been developed further than the state in which he showed them. In some cases roads were laid out, but the residential blocks on them are just the usual speculative developers' blocks, perhaps with a bit more clapboarding and some postmodernist trimmings. Duany and Plater-Zyberk's pioneering development Seaside of the late 1980s, famous also for its use as a film set in a movie, has in the meantime been overtaken in scale and ambition only by Poundbury in Dorset, the development of Charles, Prince of Wales, in his position as a major West Country landowner and using the British planning system to achieve different visual ends. It is not enough that it takes a prince to realize a fantasy; there is also a view—which I first heard from Mark Cousins at the Architectural Association, and which was developed by his student Frances Mikuriya in her doctoral dissertation on the subject—that the Prince's architectural ambitions express explicitly his desire to move into a state of retrenchment away from the modernism that he saw eating away at London in his youth during the 1950s.[6] No doubt many people felt the same: but he alone, of all of them, had the means to do something about it. Meanwhile, the timing of the current crisis in the property and housing market must in any case have stalled a great deal of New Urbanist development in the United States, and that in itself is a further marker of the tragic nature of the enterprise. The more ambitious the scheme, the less likely it was to have happened. Even the New Urbanists' more modest aims of hiding cars or camouflaging parking lots, the few things that distinguished them from modernist planners, have largely been thwarted: it is clear from aerial photographs of even relatively developed, high-end schemes—Kentlands in Maryland, for example, or Mashpee Islands on Cape Cod—that this was simply too difficult to achieve.

The New Urbanism can be seen as a large-scale retrenchment fantasy, then; it may have grown out of an ancient tradition, but it is most closely allied to a specific early-twentieth-century development of it. The whole tragic nobility of the movement does not lie in its originality,

FIGURE 5.3
Poundbury, Dorset: the model village of Charles, Prince of Wales, designed from the late 1980s onward and developed continuously ever since. Courtesy of Keith Diplock.

FIGURE 5.4
Poundbury: the detailing of houses varies as if they had been built at different periods in history, but most of them tend toward Georgian styles. Courtesy of Keith Diplock.

its style, its ambition, and least of all in its large-scale realization, for very little, if any, of these exist; instead it lies in its failure to achieve any of these to the degree where it can call itself a success. And what differentiates this failure from those of the people, the houses, and the interiors I have up to now been describing is simply the vast scale of the enterprise, the dream of creating a whole town within its own landscape, the sharing in a passion to retreat from real life and to re-create it in one's own image, but with fantastical town halls and public buildings, whole streets and boulevards of the imagination—a noble retrenchment from the pain of real life which seems to have ended, mainly, in a great deal of paper and very little else.

SUMMING UP

This book has set out to explain why architectural criticism has been so superficial for so long, and what effect this has had not only on writing itself but also on the quality of most of the buildings that are built. Mostly, writers on architecture have a sense of what is "good" and what is "bad"; they have concentrated on defining the former in ever more exclusive terms, and they have had nothing but derision for the latter. It seems an easy game to play, because every designer can hold a clear opinion about what looks to them like good-quality or even exciting work; furthermore, trained or educated designers have been indoctrinated in some form or another of dogmatic thinking. Powerful fashions come and go. But stating and restating this good–bad polarity does not do enough for improving the quality of the built environment; neither, equally significantly, does it come close to expressing the range of ideas that architects, especially unsuccessful ones, are trying to grasp at in their work, and conveying it to the public at large.

I do not believe that an architect's biography tells us anything useful about them as a designer apart, perhaps, from some sense of where they might have found their ideas. It is important to remember that ultimately it is the object, not the person, we are talking about here. But that object carries inside it a great deal of information about the motives of the designer and the place where they found themselves at the time they were working. And, as the novelist within every critic will remind us, it does not matter if we do not actually know what the architect really felt. We do not really know, in spite of some firsthand evidence, what either Thomas Ford or Percy Flaxman thought about St. Mark's church in Ramsgate. Architectural criticism is not a branch of newspaper journalism, or even necessarily an attempt to record the truth: it is there to stimulate thinking, to bring ideas together, and to engage the public in what architects do. This business about having to deal with "the truth" is nothing more than yet another hangover from the evangelical 1840s.

The example of St. Mark's came by way of explaining how even a small building—no doubt very similar to ones that we all know and see every day—has a great deal of backstory about it, pieces of information which help to build up a richer idea of what it actually means and was trying to achieve, and can draw out a narrative which enables it to reach much more of a community than first appears: in fact, a series of stories can be launched by only a brief examination of it. The impact of St. Mark's may be inspired by the sight of the building, but essentially it is a literary story about personal experience which relates more closely to how most people see architecture. To describe a building in this disjointed and scarcely visual way is closer to what successful novelists do, and we all know that their appeal to people in general is greater than that of architects and architectural writers: compare the book sales.

So that is the first point. The title of this book, *Bleak Houses*, reflects the second: the inevitably tragic nature of most places that we see and know, the bleakness that derives from the impossibility of a building to live up to its architect's own hopes, and for the architect to be proud of what he or she has done. Nearly all architectural history ignores the failures, the losers, who in many different ways are responsible for the world in which we live, and who between them provide endless new perspectives on the buildings they created. We have seen that in some cases this may have been due to their misfortune: bad temper, exile, illness, death, loss of talent, making the wrong connections. It may even have been because of something as straightforward as a lack of firsthand documentation, as happened with James Wyatt, to some extent with Horace Field, and certainly with many architects such as Percy Flaxman whose trail is almost completely obscured. Some first-rate designers have not appeared in canonical surveys because of a combination of these things; the position of Erich Mendelsohn—unquestionably one of the greatest designers in Western architectural history, certainly the first to develop a kind of built architecture that expressed modernism in the dynamic way that others only spoke about—has never been as prominent as it would have been but for the terrible combination of exile, demolition, misrepresentation, personal animosity, and early death that destroyed him stage by stage. One bleak house that has stuck in my mind is the Long Island home of John Bedenkapp, at Wainscott near East Hampton, the only project of his to have made it onto the catalog of the British Architectural Library. According to the article I found there, in an issue of *House & Garden* from June 1979, Bedenkapp's house, converted some years previously from nineteenth-century stables, was completely obliterated following remodeling by the better-known Robert Stern within a few years. The article purported to show the house both before and after the second conversion. And yet the story turns out not to be true: Stern has pointed out that the house he worked on was in fact a different one, and this is borne out by a close inspection of the photographs. So Bedenkapp's record is, first of all, misrepresented; secondly, it is in Britain represented only by one article in a lifestyle magazine; and thirdly, it is, humiliatingly, most likely only mentioned at all because the name of Stern was mistakenly associated with it. Furthermore, Bedenkapp, who died prematurely of prostate cancer, was the retiring kind too: he built his vanished house so that "he could, when he felt inclined, retire from the outside world, and retreat within a retreat, as it were."[7] The cards have been stacked up against him.

But some people are losers as architects because they did not have, or could not develop, a talent for designing buildings that appealed to others. I have suggested that they divide into at least three different types. First, there are those whose work is unsuccessful because it is within a style that is never taken seriously by critics, or by high-art architects; that it was a victim of bullying tactics from critics and editors. Secondly, there are those whose architecture has never matured, because for one reason or another they work in the kind of architectural practice that does not take design seriously, or is not bothered about keeping up to date with criticism and the work of others. These are the people who design, for example, cheap contemporary housing that is entirely lacking in any decent architectural qualities at all: it is marred by superficial decoration and formless, illogical shapemaking, and has no place in any coherent story of the development of architectural style and discipline. They are losers because there is no public discussion about what they are trying to do and what their buildings should look like. Conventional, highbrow architectural criticism does not apply to them; no doubt these architects resent such treatment as they do receive. They just go on doing what they want, perhaps to satisfy a developer who has no interest in the appearance of the building either, and no doubt in so doing they are suppressing their own latent sensitivity to beauty: a terrible thing. In order for these people to start producing buildings as satisfactory as, for example, the plainest Georgian row housing, we need to find a way of speaking about what they are doing. We need to talk about style, and how it develops. And we also need to find a way of talking about the language of doors and windows, and all the rest of it, without sounding like a textbook. Interior design magazines can do this in their way. We cannot in ours.

But then there is the third group of losers: those who know how architectural history and criticism work, but are unable to come up with the goods themselves because they are just not born with the talent for it, or perhaps the discipline for it. Architecture has a significant element of personal failure in it that is not usually recognized by conventional critics, to the extent that much that is relevant in the experience of buildings is not discussed at all. That personal failure usually relates to the relationship between the designer and their building. The fact that a person is unsuccessful in their life is not necessarily related to the history of their architecture; but the fact that their building was disappointing to them or in the opinion of others certainly is relevant, especially where the period in which they lived was hostile to them, historically, stylistically, economically. It is possible to appreciate buildings outside the conventions of architectural criticism, for example by talking about the hopes of those who design them, rather than about the actuality; since our culture is essentially a literary rather than a visual one, more people can thus be drawn into a discussion on what a building is trying to do and what it is about. Here too, everything that I have said above is relevant: try first to talk about the aims and memories of the architects; ask them "What are you trying to do?" Try to make their answers into the story that guides the building, as indeed you would with a high-art designer without finding it odd to do so. Architectural writing is unnecessarily brutal and judgmental, and does not relate much anyhow to the way in which most people see buildings.

REAL LIFE

The clues about how to do this, in writing and in teaching, lie in real life. Some architectural traditions have been suppressed by critics because they were about beauty, joy, retiral, comfort, coziness; there is no reason related to human nature why this suppression should have come about, and at certain times—in the 1820s and 1830s, and exactly a century later—architectural writers were not ashamed to say that they enjoyed these things. People enjoy beauty, which is not so indefinable or subjective as is often thought. But, more usefully, most people also enjoy sentimentality; architecture critics, and especially teachers, seem to dislike this more than anything else, in spite of the fact that sentiment often has a useful narrative quality to it which can be used to give parts of a building different voices for different times, and to express combinations of personal failure and triumph in ways that other people can understand. The unnecessary conflation of sentiment and feeling with kitsch has done a great disservice to those narrative qualities of architecture that potentially enable it to communicate with nonprofessionals. In fact buildings have within themselves many contradictions—contradictions which express what is going on within them, and also the transient nature of some of the activities as compared to the permanence of others; interior designers understand this, but the architects everyone has heard of do not. There is a difference between consistency and coherence, and a building can be coherent while being full of contradictions. Very often the story of the building lies precisely in this contradiction, not in any of the more usual conventions of architecture; and the impossible yearning for lost life that one sometimes feels in looking through old and unfashionable books on architecture, that unhappiness at the conflict between past memories and present needs, is a strong emotion that should be recorded somewhere. In fact, when architecture appears in places other than in real buildings or architects' fantasies—for example, in both highbrow and popular novels—it sometimes has more to say than architecture critics can manage when they talk about the real thing: these literary buildings can look back, remember, regret, link into personal experience and narrative. As Roger Scruton wrote in his *Beauty: A Very Short Introduction*:

> The judgement of beauty is not just an optional addition to the repertoire of human judgements, but the unavoidable consequence of taking life seriously, and becoming truly conscious of our affairs.[8]

I mentioned in my introduction that my former student Adam Summerfield, himself a talented designer, suggested that non-architects might understand architects' ideas better if they heard the story behind them and understood the kind of world the designers were trying to create in literary terms, rather than through an exhibition of drawings and sophisticated animations: an observation that arose following the exhibition of an ambitious master plan for the riverfront in the deprived, historic Kent town of Chatham. At the launch of the show, the architects and promoters were excited; but local residents were appalled. The story that the people of Chatham needed might have been about any one of a number of things, or about a combination of several of them not necessarily connected: it might have been about river breezes or a pleasant view; it might have been the history of the place, or the arrival on the scene of a Dutch invasion fleet in 1667; about the military life of the town that has ebbed away; about building the Victorian civic center that never actually existed. It might have been a story with a plot, apparently unrelated to the design of the buildings: a detective story, a historical romance, a modern thriller. It might even have been, trivially but more realistically, about the places the architects had seen on their holidays and wanted to re-create here in a different place, at a different time. For more interesting, and more important to any architectural writer who wants to explain the buildings to those who will live with them, are the stories about what the architects wanted to do: which dreams they were living out, and which memories they wanted to recall. Which of their successes they were celebrating, and which of their disasters they were trying to forget.

How they related to the old buildings of the town, and how they wanted to build on them. These are things that can be conveyed to non-architects. None of these stories would have detracted from the quality of the architecture that a decent architect would have designed for the site, and there is some hope that they might have contributed to it. Without a common language we are destined to go on churning out ugly houses and fighting a lack of comprehension on the part of most of society. We have, in other words, insufficient architecture culture as part of our culture as a whole.

DROWNING IN LONELINESS

Life is a battle for most people; some are lucky enough to be able to translate that battle into a creative experience, but most architects face the horror of realizing that they have no real ability or opportunity to create that cathartic, imagined thing out of what has gone wrong with their life or career. That "thing" might be a piece of furniture or a single room, the first projects we were given to do when we arrived at architecture school, or it might be a whole town; either way, from the first moment of confronting the project there might be a feeling that what is required by the current architectural world is beyond you. These are the strongest emotions that any designer can feel, quite equal to any of the other few major passions in life: love; fear; jealousy; hunger; physical pain. There is a feeling these failing people sometimes have that they want to draw back, sink away into obscurity, retreat from the world and create one of their own that is more to their liking; to force the reality of what they see around them into a place that is more congenial—to force, as it were, the pale lilac heather into becoming the lucky white variety, however pathetic the ambition: a feeling of drowning, of wondering whether or not to fight the lack of consciousness that comes over them; whether to surrender; whether to slip into retrenchment and forgetfulness. It can happen to you at any stage of your career.

I write about this subject with some feeling, because I was cursed enough to want to be a designer with the discipline, but without enough creative talent, to do it as well as I wanted. I had a sense of what worked well, what was constructionally logical, what was well planned and what functioned efficiently, and furthermore I could tell the story of what I wanted to do with any given project; but I always knew, whenever I saw the white heather of the talented designers in my year at architecture school, that I was not going to be one of them. I found that I was often making excuses for my lack of ability to stretch myself—that it was to do with personal loneliness, with personal rejection, all the other big things that life throws up. I could read but I could not concentrate; I did not think purely in visual terms in the way that real designers do. I also had a natural sense of not wanting to belong to cliques and groups, and I was held back by my own sentimental idea of what I wanted a building to be about, as I still am when I hover over my old books, with their Edwardian images of pergolas and paneled rooms. All these are excuses for a lack of talent. And yet I think I could have been saved as a designer if there had been some kind of broad architectural community that I could have shared a language with, and I found this in my own reading of the buildings around me rather than in highbrow architectural circles. If there is one thing that architecture schools could do, it would be to talk much more about the story of each student's proposed building, try to tease out what exactly the intention behind it should be, and then look for a logical, tectonic, and constructional way of creating it. The whole of architectural history is, after all, standing by at our shoulders trying to help. At a certain point, the talking should turn into the discipline of construction. These are the things we need to do to get a comprehensive architecture culture going. And nothing here will in any way damage the quality of the buildings that the talented people do produce: they will go on doing their thing, if they are lucky, because it comes directly out of their sense of being alive. They will, mostly, find their champions. We don't have to worry about them.

In Muriel Spark's short story "The Go-Away Bird," a story which draws its theme from the call of a South African bird that sounds as if it is telling those around it to get lost, the young exploited heroine Daphne, out on the arid veldt, endlessly brushed aside by others, dreams of a life among the riverbanks and greenery of a lush English countryside. She gets near to it when she is engaged to a flight lieutenant in the Royal Air Force who tells her, of his family home by the River Thames in Berkshire, that "the water simply walks over the garden"; after he is killed, only a week later, "she felt that the garden had gone under the sea."[9] I read this for the first time on a District Line Underground train as it came into Richmond station in 1985, when I was a student living nearby, and I remember something else about that journey too. I saw a father—he looked a kindly sort of man—holding the hand of his young son, perhaps four or five years old, the two of them gazing into each other's eyes. Because I had never had a father like that, and because I would never have the chance to hold a son like that either, I felt as if the floor of the railway carriage was slipping away from under my feet. I knew what the limitations of my talent were, and I think I hoped that my own future buildings, the ones I would try to excuse by saying that I was doing as I was told at school or in the office, or blamed on an awkward site, or unpromising circumstances, or lack of money—the projects that would be simply the demonstrations to the outside world of my own lack of talent—would compensate me by becoming somehow my own children, my own disappointing offspring that I could love in spite of their clumsiness and stupidity; and yet I knew that this would not be so. I had not yet learned to leave the children thing to the virile. The feeling that I had every morning when the sun rose yet again magnificent, and the birds sang, and the leaves on the many trees in Richmond's verdant avenues rustled and beckoned as they celebrated the exhilaration of another day, was that perhaps there would eventually be a chance to get things right, that I would be recognized; and yet nothing seemed to happen. In the song which is perhaps the greatest epiphonic anthem of all time, and which then reverberated through department store loudspeakers, in elevators, in workshops, and through the windows of passing cars, I heard the voice of the singer Barry Manilow as it rose and fell in ecstasy, forever insistent; tenaciously optimistic: "Could this be the magic at last?" No, it isn't. It never will be. And in the meantime you can come and find me sitting alone in Horace Field's pretty rose garden in Surrey, opposite the pious inscription over his front door—or, at least, you could have done had it not been uprooted and replaced in the meantime by an ugly extension.

NOTES

INTRODUCTION

1. Quoted in Margaret Belcher, *The Collected Letters of A. W. N. Pugin*, vol. 2 (Oxford: Oxford University Press, 2003), 16–17.

2. For realism or "reality," see Chris Brooks, *The Gothic Revival* (London: Phaidon, 1999), 305.

3. Voysey described his aims in building as "reverence, love, justice, mercy, honesty, candour, generosity, humility, loyalty, order, and dignity," to quote a typical sequence from his book *Individuality* (C. F. A. Voysey, *Individuality* [London: Chapman & Hall, 1915], 11); Libeskind's choice of vocabulary has increasingly been lampooned, notably by Miles Glendinning, for example in his *Architecture's Evil Empire: The Triumph and Tragedy of Global Modernism* (London: Reaktion, 2010), 123.

4. Adam Summerfield, "Rethinking Medway—a Proposal for Democratic Participation in the Development of Chatham Waterfront," undergraduate dissertation, University of Kent, Canterbury, 2008.

5. C. F. A. Voysey, "Ideas in Things," in *The Arts Connected with Building*, ed. T. Raffles Davison (London: Batsford, 1909), 101–137.

6. Described in Alison Lurie, *Not in Front of the Grown-Ups* (London: Sphere Books, 1991), 68.

7. Nikolaus Pevsner, *The Buildings of England: London: Volume One, The Cities of London and Westminster* (Harmondsworth: Penguin, 1973), footnote, 183.

8. English Heritage rejection note 473855, dated November 19, 2012.

9. See Timothy Brittain-Catlin, "Downward Trajectory: Towards a Theory of Failure," *Architecture Research Quarterly* 15, no. 3 (2011): 139–147.

10. A. Stuart Gray, *Edwardian Architecture: A Biographical Dictionary* (London: Duckworth, 1985), 178.

11. Bill Fawcett, *The North Eastern Railway's Two Palaces of Business* (York: Friends of the National Railway Museum, 2001); see also Timothy Brittain-Catlin, "Horace Field and Lloyds Bank," *Architectural History* 53 (2010): 271–294.

12. Roger Cunliffe, in conversation with the author in November 2010. He told me that both he and the primary designer of the building, Stirrat Johnson-Marshall, had always intended it to be a temporary exhibition pavilion—that was the whole point of it, he said.

13. In "Ideas in Things," C. F. A. Voysey wrote about this at some length; for example: "At sunset we see horizontal lines as if all nature were reclining and preparing for rest, dim light drawing a veil over disturbing detail" (Voysey, "Ideas in Things," 115). Pevsner, by contrast, wrote of Voysey's Broadleys of 1898: "from this centre bay with its completely unmoulded mullions and transoms, from these windows cut clean and sheer into the wall, access to the architectural style of today [1936] could have been direct, more direct probably than from the designs of those few in England who in the late nineties appeared more revolutionary than Voysey" (Nikolaus Pevsner, *Pioneers of Modern Design: From William Morris to Walter Gropius* [Harmondsworth: Penguin, 1960], 162). Pevsner was of course right, and Voysey either wrong or dissimulating.

14. See Andrew Dolkart, *The Row House Reborn: Architecture and Neighborhoods in New York City, 1908–1929* (Baltimore: Johns Hopkins University Press, 2009).

15. Reyner Banham, "The Style: 'Flimsy . . . Effeminate?,'" in *A Tonic to the Nation: The Festival of Britain 1951*, ed. Mary Banham and Bevis Hillier (London: Thames & Hudson, 1976), 193.

16. For example, in Deyan Sudjic, *Norman Foster: A Life in Architecture* (London: Weidenfeld & Nicolson, 2010).

17. Francesco Dal Co, Kurt W. Forster, and Arnold Hadley, *Frank O. Gehry: The Complete Works* (New York: Monacelli Press, 1998), 19.

18. Paul Oliver, Ian Davis, and Ian Bentley, *Dunroamin: The Suburban Semi and Its Enemies* (London: Barrie & Jenkins, 1981); Gavin Stamp, "Neo-Tudor and Its Enemies," *Architectural History* 49 (2006): 1–33.

19. Andrew Ballantyne and Andrew Law, *Tudoresque: In Pursuit of the Ideal Home* (London: Reaktion, 2011).

20. Alex Ross, *The Rest Is Noise: Listening to the Twentieth Century* (London: Harper Perennial, 2009), 417.

21. *Guardian*, March 30, 2007: see http://www.guardian.co.uk/stage/theatreblog/2007/mar/30/onstagenudityletsgrowupno.

CHAPTER 1

1. Nitza Metzger-Szmuk, *Batim min hachol: adrikhalut hasignon habeinleumi beTel Aviv, 1931–1948* (Tel Aviv: Ministry of Defense, 1994), 146.

2. These are described in Bill Fawcett, *The North Eastern Railway's Two Palaces of Business* (York: Friends of the National Railway Museum, 2001), 47–56.

3. Timothy Brittain-Catlin, "Horace Field and Lloyds Bank," *Architectural History* 53 (2010): 271–294, passim.

4. Horace Field and Michael Bunney, *English Domestic Architecture of the XVII and XVIII Centuries: A Selection of Examples of Smaller Buildings / Measured, Drawn and*

Photographed, with an Introduction and Notes by Horace Field and Michael Bunney (London: George Bell, 1905; 2nd edn. 1928).

5. This was my conclusion when researching "Horace Field and Lloyds Bank": see 284.

6. Horace Field, "Architectural Reminiscences—no. 14," *The Builder* (October 11, 1946): 370.

7. See Timothy Brittain-Catlin, "Downward Trajectory: Towards a Theory of Failure," *Architecture Research Quarterly* 15, no. 3 (2011): 139–147.

8. Lawrence Weaver, *Small Country Houses of To-day* (London: Country Life, 1911), 48.

9. Nikolaus Pevsner, Elizabeth Williamson, and Geoffrey K. Brandwood, *The Buildings of England: Buckinghamshire* (London: Penguin, 1994), 164.

10. Jean-Marie Rouart, *La noblesse des vaincus* (Paris: Grasset, 1997).

11. *Die Architekten*, directed by Peter Kahane and produced by DEFA; East Germany, 1989–1990.

12. The recurrent theme of Jeremy Till, *Architecture Depends* (Cambridge, Mass: MIT Press, 2009), but also in his earlier writing, for example "The Architecture of the Impure Community," in *Occupying Architecture: Between the Architect and the User*, ed. Jonathan Hill (London: Routledge, 1998).

13. Niels L. Prak, *Architects: The Noted and the Ignored* (Chichester: John Wiley & Sons, 1984), especially 12–14.

14. Howard Colvin, *A Biographical Dictionary of British Architects 1600–1840* (New Haven: Yale University Press, 1995), 417.

15. Frank Lloyd Wright, *An Autobiography* (London: Quartet, 1977), 90–92.

16. Ibid., 154–155.

17. Alan Hess and Alan Weintraub, *The Architecture of John Lautner* (London: Thames & Hudson, 1999), 29, 31, 33.

18. Jane Ridley, *The Architect and His Wife: A Life of Edwin Lutyens* (London: Chatto & Windus, 2002), 396.

19. Gavin Stamp, *An Architect of Promise: George Gilbert Scott Junior (1839–1897) and the Late Gothic Revival* (Donington: Shaun Tyas, 2002), 329–331, 341.

20. For the syphilis claim, see Christabel Powell, *Augustus Pugin, Designer of the British Houses of Parliament* (Lampeter: Edwin Mellen Press, 2006), 9, for what seems to be the first published reference; the hypothesis is a significant theme in the later chapters of Rosemary Hill, *God's Architect: Pugin and the Building of Romantic Britain* (London: Penguin, 2007). For Edward Pugin, see Catriona Blaker, *Edward Pugin and Kent* (Ramsgate: Pugin Society, 2003), 60–61; Gerard Hyland, "Edward Welby Pugin, Architect, 1834–75," *True Principles, the Journal of the Pugin Society* 4, no. 1 (Autumn 2009): 51–55.

21. Gerard Hyland, "The E. W. Pugin Gazetteer Part 2," *True Principles, the Journal of the Pugin Society* 3, no. 5 (Autumn 2008): 48.

22. Christopher Spencer and Geoffrey Wilson, *Elbow Room: The Story of John Sydney Brocklesby, Arts and Crafts Architect* (London: Ainsworth and Nelson in conjunction with Christopher Spencer, Graystones Press and Dasprint Ltd., 1984), 47.

23. Louise Kehoe, *In This Dark House* (Harmondsworth: Penguin, 1997), for example 48–52.

24. For Utzon and the Opera House, see Andrew Saint, *Architect and Engineer: A Study in Sibling Rivalry* (New Haven: Yale University Press, 2007), 371–377; for Zunz, ibid., 377.

25. Quoted in Regina Stephan, "One of the Most Lovable People and at the Same Time One of the Most Unpleasant: Mendelsohn and His Assistants in the 1920s and Early 1930s," in Stephan, ed., *Erich Mendelsohn, Dynamics and Function: Realized Visions of a Cosmopolitan Architect* (Ostfildern-Ruit: IFA, 1999), 156.

26. Walter Gropius seems to have been the most vicious of them: see Kathleen James, *Erich Mendelsohn and the Architecture of German Modernism* (Cambridge: Cambridge University Press, 1997), 246.

27. Ita Heinze-Greenberg, "We'll Leave It to the Schultzes from Naumburg to Ignore the Mediterranean as the Father of the International Art of Composition," in Stephan, ed., *Erich Mendelsohn*, 189.

28. Elizabeth Darling, *Wells Coates* (London: RIBA Publishing, 2012), 99–105 (BBC), 143–151 (gazetteer).

29. John Martin Robinson, *James Wyatt, 1746–1813: Architect to George III* (London: Paul Mellon Centre for Studies in British Art, 2012), especially xi–xii, 20, 303.

30. Stamp, *Architect of Promise*, 295.

31. Nikolaus Pevsner, "Goodhart-Rendel's Roll-Call," in *Edwardian Architecture and Its Origins*, ed. Alastair Service (London: Architectural Press, 1975), 479.

32. Obituary by Edwin Johnson, *Architectural Review* (July 1991): 9.

33. Peter Blundell Jones, email to author, November 13, 2012. For a detailed account of Hübner, see Peter Blundell Jones, *Peter Hübner: Building as a Social Process / Peter Hübner: Bauen als sozialer Prozeß* (Fellbach: Axel Menges, 2007).

34. My thanks to Björn Ehrlemark for this: he adds that there is a dissertation on Wallberg in Swedish from 1993, but not much else.

35. Chris Foges, "Making Sense of Place," *Architecture Today* (October 2012): 8–11. One of Gordon's buildings, the now demolished Trinity Square car park in Gateshead, northeast England, of 1962, achieved cult status for its role in the Michael Caine film *Get Carter* (1971).

36. David Watkin, *Visions of World Architecture* (London: Sir John Soane's Museum, 2007), 15.

37. Christopher Webster, *R. D. Chantrell (1793–1872) and the Architecture of a Lost Generation* (Reading: Spire, 2010); Margaret Belcher, *The Collected Letters of A. W. N. Pugin*, vol. 2 (Oxford: Oxford University Press, 2003), 252, 288–289.

38. Colvin, *Biographical Dictionary*, 278–279. See Diana Burfield, *Edward Cresy 1792–1858: Architect and Civil Engineer* (Donington: Shaun Tyas, 2003) for the full story.

39. Timothy Brittain-Catlin, *The English Parsonage in the Early Nineteenth Century* (Reading: Spire, 2008), 200–210.

40. Malcolm Borg, *British Colonial Architecture, Malta 1800–1900* (San Gwann, Malta: Publishers Enterprise Group, 2001), 44–49.

41. Described in Susan Hattis Rolef, "The Knesset Building in Giv'at Ram—Planning and Construction," originally published in Hebrew in *Cathedra (Journal for Holy Land Studies)* 96, Yad Izhak Ben-Zvi, Jerusalem, July 2002; English language version available at http://www.knesset.gov.il/building/architecture/eng/article1_eng.htm.

42. This was how Ya'aqov Rechter described him to me, to my astonishment, in a conversation in the mid-1990s.

43. Charles Saumarez Smith, *The Building of Castle Howard* (London: Faber & Faber, 1990), 70.

44. Ibid., 184.

45. Charles Jencks, *Modern Movements in Architecture* (Harmondsworth: Penguin, 1973), 20–25.

46. Timothy Brittain-Catlin, *Leonard Manasseh and Partners* (London: RIBA Publishing, 2010), 80–85.

47. The architect of this recent remodeling was Ram Karmi, one of those who had displaced Klarwein at the Knesset 50 years earlier. According to the *HaAretz* newspaper on October 11, 2010, Karmi's response to critics of his new design was they could "kiss my ass": http://www.haaretz.com/print-edition/business/habima-architect-tells-critics-kiss-my-ass-1.318315.

48. Myra Wahrhaftig, *They Laid the Foundation: Lives and Works of German-Speaking Jewish Architects in Palestine 1918–1948* (Berlin: Wasmuth, 2007), 158–160.

49. I am grateful to Ellis Woodman for drawing my attention to Reynolds, who in his opinion provided some of the inspiration behind Stirling and Gowan's Leicester University Engineering Faculty building. My sincere thanks to Edward Bottoms, archivist at the AA, for kindly providing documentation on Reynolds, including his obituary: W. G. Howell, "Edward Reynolds," *Architectural Association Journal* (February 1959): 218.

50. So his doctors told the *Architects' Journal* (February 5, 1986): 17. Richmond apartments: *Architects' Journal* (September 26, 1935): 449–450, 453–457. Ray Cecil wrote monthly about the emerging legal dangers for architects in the *RIBA Journal* from the mid-1980s. *Times* obituary: February 5, 1986.

CHAPTER 2

1. Nikolaus Pevsner and Bill Wilson, *Norfolk 2: North West and South* (London: Penguin, 1999), 683.

2. See Adam Menuge, *Oxburgh Hall, Oxborough, Norfolk: A Survey and Investigation of the Moated House* (London: English Heritage, 2006), for a full description of the building.

3. http://www.catholicparish-swaffham.org.uk/index.php?module=pagesmith&id=38.

4. Peter Blundell Jones, "Richmond Riverside: Sugaring the Pill," *Architectural Review* (November 1988): 90.

5. For a recent overview of the *Essex Design Guide*, see Elain Harwood and Alan Powers, "From Downtown to Diversity: Revisiting the 1970s," in *Twentieth Century Architecture 10: The Seventies*, ed. Elain Harwood and Alan Powers (London: Twentieth Century Society, 2012), 22–24.

6. Matthew Habershon, *The Ancient Half-Timbered Houses of England* (London: John Weale, 1836–1839). For St. James' Cathedral, Mount Zion, see Howard Colvin, *A Biographical Dictionary of British Architects 1600–1840* (New Haven: Yale University Press, 1995), 442, 547.

7. Mark Girouard, *Elizabethan Architecture: Its Rise and Fall, 1540–1640* (New Haven: Yale University Press for the Paul Mellon Centre for British Art, 2009).

8. A. W. N. Pugin, *Contrasts, or a Parallel between the Noble Edifices of the Middle Ages, and the Corresponding buildings of the Present day; shewing the Present Decay of Taste*, 2nd edn. (London: Charles Dolman, 1841), 65.

9. Alfred Bartholomew, *Specifications for Practical Architecture, Preceded by an Essay on the Decline of Excellence in the Structure and in the Science of Modern English Buildings, with the Proposal of Remedies for those Defects* (London: John Williams, 1840), I-XVIII-623.

10. Ibid., I-LXVIII-632.

11. Ibid., I-LXXIII-641.

12. Joseph Gwilt, *An Encyclopaedia of Architecture, Historical, Theoretical and Practical* (London: Longman, Brown, Green, and Longman, 1842), §437, 195.

13. For Tudor massing and details on a neoclassical style, see Averham rectory, Nottinghamshire, in Timothy Brittain-Catlin, *The English Parsonage in the Early Nineteenth Century* (Reading: Spire, 2008), 110, fig. 2.57; for transgendered architecture, and in particular Norton vicarage in Hertfordshire, see ibid., 112–113, figs. 2.63–2.64.

14. See ibid., passim.

15. Devey: see Jill Allibone, *George Devey Architect, 1820–1886* (Cambridge, UK: Lutterworth Press, 1991), especially 135, 141. Shaw: see Andrew Saint, *Richard Norman Shaw* (New Haven: Yale University Press, 2010), 105–106.

16. Peter Mandler, *The Fall and Rise of the Stately Home* (New Haven: Yale University Press, 1997), part one chapter one, "The Victorian Idea of Heritage," 20–69.

17. P. H. Ditchfield, *The Charm of the English Village* (London: Batsford, 1908), 40.

18. P. H. Ditchfield, *The Manor Houses of England* (London: Batsford, 1910), 3–4.

19. Oliver, Davis & Bentley, *Dunroamin*; Stamp, "Neo-Tudor"; Ballantyne and Law, *Tudoresque*; and John Betjeman's BBC film *Metro-land* (directed and produced by Edward Mirzoeff, 1972–1973).

20. Thomas Garner, *The Domestic Architecture of England During the Tudor Period*, with an introduction by Arthur Stratton (London: Batsford, 1911), vi.

21. Pugin, *Contrasts*, 57. Original emphasis.

22. A. W. N. Pugin, *An Apology for the Revival of Christian Architecture* (London: John Weale, 1843), footnote, 3.

23. Ibid., 15–16. See also Bartholomew, *Specifications*, I-XLII-384.

24. Vanbrugh, on seeing the name of the talentless neo-Palladian architect Thomas Ripley in a newspaper: "such a Laugh came upon me, I had like to Beshit myself" (Colvin, *Biographical Dictionary*, 819). But this was a private comment.

25. Alan Hollinghurst, *The Stranger's Child* (London: Picador, 2011), 8.

26. Ibid., 8, 15, 29.

27. J. C. Loudon, *An Encyclopaedia of Cottage, Farm, and Villa Architecture and Furniture* (London: Longman, 1833), section 1338, 621.

28. Elizabeth Bowen, *Eva Trout* (London: Vintage, 1999), 79–80.

29. Alexandra Harris, *Romantic Moderns: English Writers, Artists and the Imagination from Virginia Woolf to John Piper* (London: Thames & Hudson, 2010), 56–57, 266–271.

30. Michael Cunningham, *By Nightfall* (London: Fourth Estate, 2010), 178–181.

31. H. S. Goodhart-Rendel, *English Architecture since the Regency. An Interpretation* (London: Constable, 1953), 225.

32. Helena Gerrish, *Edwardian Country Life: The Story of H. Avray Tipping* (London: Frances Lincoln, 2011), 52.

33. According to the chart published in the *Guardian* newspaper, December 29, 2013, and compiled on the basis of figures supplied by Nielsen BookScan, the autobiography of the entertainer and celebrity Cheryl Cole had sold 223,358 copies since its publication the previous October; by contrast, Mark Girouard's *Elizabethan Architecture*, an accessible work of great scholarship produced by one of Britain's finest and most influential architectural writers on the basis of a lifetime's study, and illustrated with photography by the late Martin Charles, often described as the country's most outstanding architectural photographer, had sold about 3,000 copies since its publication in Fall 2009 (figure from Yale University Press, January 2013). Cole's book was therefore selling at a monthly rate of about 1,000 times that of Girouard's.

34. Vincent Scully, "The Architecture of Community," in Peter Katz, *The New Urbanism: Toward an Architecture of Community* (New York: McGraw-Hill, 1994), 228.

35. Kenneth Powell, "Erith in Context," in *Raymond Erith: Progressive Classicist 1904–1973*, ed. Lucy Archer (London: Sir John Soane's Museum, 2004), 23.

36. Ibid., 19.

37. Mark Lamster, "181 Renoirs, 69 Cézannes, 59 Matisses and 46 Picassos," *Architectural Review* (August 2012): 60. In his recent interview with Chris Foges, the British critic Jonathan Meades deployed Wyndham Lewis's comment that the Sitwell family of writers "were part of the history of publicity, not the history of literature" to suggest that the same applied to some well-known architects (in his opinion, Alvar Aalto, James Stirling, and the Smithsons): Chris Foges, "Making Sense of Place," *Architecture Today* (October 2012): 10.

38. In Owen Williams, "Architecture—Trade, Profession or Calling," *Architectural Association Journal* (January 1953): 102.

39. See Peter Blundell Jones, "Between Tradition and Modernity: The Reticent Architecture of David Lea," *Spazio e Società*, no. 55 (October/December 1991); Peter Blundell Jones, "Traditional Values," *Architectural Review* (August 1993).

40. Elain Harwood and Alan Powers, *Tayler and Green Architects 1938–1973: The Spirit of Place in Modern Housing* (London: The Prince of Wales's Institute of Architecture, 1998), 66.

CHAPTER 3

1. "Architecture cannot be divorced from social and political concerns," wrote Peter Davey in the *Architectural Review* of October 1981, 204, establishing his manifesto for his editorship.

2. J. M. Richards, *Memoirs of an Unjust Fella* (London: Weidenfeld & Nicolson, 1980), 118. Elain Harwood and Alan Powers have recently concluded that Hastings's interest in architecture "was always political": Elain Harwood and Alan Powers, "From Downtown to Diversity: Revisiting the 1970s," in *Twentieth Century Architecture 10: The Seventies*, ed. Elain Harwood and Alan Powers (London: Twentieth Century Society, 2012), 11.

3. Richards, *Unjust Fella*, 90; *Architects' Journal* (March 15, 1934): 379.

4. Letter, *Architects' Journal* (January 24, 1935): 159–160.

5. When he spoke against the modernist principle of the comprehensive redevelopment of city centers, at the annual discourse of the Royal Institute of British Architects (RIBA). See J. M. Richards, "The Hollow Victory: 1932–1972," *RIBA Journal* (May 1972): 192–197.

6. Richards, *Unjust Fella*, 134.

7. For my view of the process by which British Scandinavianism was born, see Timothy Brittain-Catlin, "Gunnar Asplund, by Peter Blundell Jones," *AA files*, no. 53 (2006): 77–82.

8. See John Newman, *The Buildings of England: North East and East Kent* (Harmondsworth: Penguin, 1983), 386.

9. Alan Powers, for Casson's entry in the *Oxford Dictionary of National Biography* (online only, for subscribers).

10. Alison Smithson, "House in Soho," *Architectural Design* (December 1953): 342; original emphasis. This was given as an important source soon afterward in Reyner Banham's seminal "The New Brutalism," *Architectural Review* (December 1955): 856–857, and its significance is emphasized by the fact that it was still being cited more than 50 years later, for example in Laurent Stadler, "'New Brutalism', 'Topology' and 'Image': Some Remarks on the Architectural Debates in England around 1950," *Journal of Architecture* 13, no. 3 (June 2008): 264–265.

11. Peter Ahrends, who with his partners Paul Korelek and Richard Burton was a devoted former student and admirer of the Scandinavianist Leonard Manasseh, told

me in a conversation of January 2010 that, nevertheless, the first new British building that really excited him was Stirling and Gowan's Brutalist Engineering Faculty at Leicester, completed in 1963.

12. Kenneth Frampton, *Modern Architecture: A Critical History* (London: Thames & Hudson, 1985), 262.

13. Ibid., 264.

14. We noticed on a recent visit that the only person flashing a cock at Coventry is Epstein's Devil, directed at visitors rising up along the main entrance steps.

15. Frampton, *Modern Architecture*, 264.

16. Alan Powers, *Britain* (London: Reaktion, 2007), 99. Powers refers to Frampton's argument that there was no logical point of comparison between the type of traditional housing that the Smithsons admired, and the housing they designed themselves that was supposed to be related to it (109). Andrew Higgott, *Mediating Modernism: Architectural Cultures in Britain* (Abingdon: Routledge, 2007), chapter 4, provides a detailed description of the impact of the Smithsons and growth of Brutalism and its context in British architectural writing and publishing.

17. In Chris Foges, "Making Sense of Place," *Architecture Today* (October 2012): 10.

18. Quoted in Barnabas Calder, "'A Terrible Battle with Architecture': Denys Lasdun in the 1950s, Part 2," *Architectural Research Quarterly* 12, no. 1 (2008): 59.

19. Charles Jencks, *Modern Movements in Architecture* (Harmondsworth: Penguin, 1973), 20–25, 245.

20. Feeble: Reyner Banham, "The Style: 'Flimsy . . . Effeminate?,'" in *A Tonic to the Nation: The Festival of Britain 1951*, ed. Mary Banham and Bevis Hillier (London: Thames & Hudson, 1976), 193, quoting from Lionel Brett, "Detail on the South Bank," *Design*, no. 32 (1951): 5; landscaping: Banham, "The Style," 197–198.

21. Peter Davey, "Outrage: Blue Blob in Birmingham," *Architectural Review* (October 2003): 24; Ed Dorrel, "Future Systems' Selfridges under Attack over Lack of Natural Lighting," *Architects' Journal* (July 10, 2003): 12.

22. Kieran Long, "Do Malls Really Excite Us Any More?," *Icon* (September 2003): 129.

23. *Building Design* (anonymous; July 22, 2005): 5.

24. Damian Arnold, "Jan Wanted to Do Extraordinary Things," *Architects' Journal* (January 22, 2009): 11. In contrast to the many attacks, the perceptive and fair Ellis Woodman, writing in *Building Design*, found Kaplický's Selfridges unexpectedly "terrific," and Alan Phillips, in *Architecture Today*, was also sympathetic: Ellis Woodman, "Bull Market," *Building Design* (September 5, 2003): 17; Alan Phillips, "Spoken into the Bloid," *Architecture Today* (October 2003). Jonathan Glancey was also sympathetic: Kaplický was in his opinion "intelligent and gifted and interesting company; he 'dared to be different,' and I think this made many architects and critics (often a very conservative bunch) treat him unkindly": email to author, October 23, 2012.

25. Kenneth Powell, *Edward Cullinan Architects* (London: Academy Editions, 1995), 47. My colleague Gerald Adler, who worked for the office in the 1980s, recalls long walks through Irish bogs as a form of social bonding.

26. Miles Glendinning, *Architecture's Evil Empire: The Triumph and Tragedy of Global Modernism* (London: Reaktion, 2010), is, overall, a recent critique of this.

27. Foges, "Making Sense," 8.

28. See Caroline Dakers, *The Holland Park Circle: Artists in Victorian Society* (New Haven: Yale University Press, 1999), 45–46; Mark Girouard, *Sweetness and Light: The "Queen Anne" Movement 1860–1900* (Oxford: Oxford University Press, 1977), 4–5; Bridget Cherry and Nikolaus Pevsner, *The Buildings of England: London 3: North West* (New Haven: Yale University Press, 2002), 503.

29. Girouard, *Sweetness and Light*, 1.

30. Clough Williams-Ellis, *England and the Octopus* (London: Godfrey Bles, 1928), unnumbered plate.

31. See Timothy Brittain-Catlin, "Downward Trajectory: Towards a Theory of Failure," *Architecture Research Quarterly* 15, no. 3 (2011): 144–145.

32. See Timothy Brittain-Catlin, "Horace Field and Lloyds Bank," *Architectural History* 53 (2010): 282, 287–288; figs. 9, 19.

33. E. F. Benson, *Mapp and Lucia* (London: Penguin, 2004), 33.

34. Clive Aslet, "An Interview with the Late Paul Paget 1901–1985," *Thirties Society Journal*, no. 6 (1987): 16. Wellington: the practice was called Gerald Wellesley and Trenwith Wills, and various high-society homosexuals—"Chips" Channon, Lord Berners—were among their clients. Wellesley succeeded his nephew to the dukedom in 1943 and died in 1972.

35. Gavin Stamp, *The Great Perspectivists* (London: Trefoil Books, 1982), and David Dean, *The Thirties: Recalling the English Architectural Scene* (London: Trefoil, 1983), mark the start of the process which has been carried on most notably since by Alan Powers and members of the Twentieth Century Society. "The Thirties," a major retrospective exhibition of the decade at the Hayward Gallery in 1979, was still mainly modernist in tone, and had little of other styles in it.

36. In the former Terry's shop at St Helen's Square, by Lewis Wade, 1923–1924 (Nikolaus Pevsner and David Neave, *The Buildings of England: Yorkshire: York and the East Riding* [New Haven: Yale University Press, 2005], 230), although in fact the Quality Street brand originated with another manufacturer, Mackintosh's of Halifax. The guide calls the style of the shop "Baroque revival," but the ironwork surely is "Queen Anne."

37. Information from the author's conversation with Rupert Butler, May 2009, and his email of January 7, 2013. For the range of examples, see http://www.superquick.co.uk.

38. Durden's granddaughter, the artist Janet Durden Hey, kindly identified the figures for me; her father was the boy at the window. Email to author, January 18, 2013.

39. Osbert Lancaster, *A Cartoon History of Architecture* (London: John Murray, 1975), 162. This observation and the reference to "Curzon Street Baroque" below were originally published in Lancaster's *Homes Sweet Homes* (London: John Murray, 1953).

40. Hugh Walpole, *Rogue Herries* (London: Frances Lincoln, 2008), 480.

41. Ibid., 185, 105.

42. For morbidity, see note 54 below.

43. Rupert Hart-Davis, *Hugh Walpole: A Biography* (London: Macmillan, 1952). Walpole's recent entry in the much more recent *Oxford Dictionary of National Biography* supplies no further information about his private life.

44. Aslet, "Paul Paget," 16. In 1947 Seely succeeded to the peerage with the title of 2nd Baron Mottistone, but the name of the practice did not change. "Partners": Eddie Anderson, Paget's stepson, in an email to the author, July 8, 2010.

45. Eddie Anderson, in conversation with the author, August 22, 2010.

46. Aslet, "Paul Paget," 19.

47. Timothy Brittain-Catlin, "Cabin Class," *The World of Interiors* (April 2009).

48. Williams-Ellis, *England and the Octopus*, 79.

49. Lancaster, *Cartoon History*, 132–133. For a full description of the old and new parts of the palace, see Christopher Hussey, "Eltham Hall," *Country Life* (May 15, 1937): 534–539; (May 22, 1937): 568–573; (May 29, 1937): 594–599.

50. The historian G. M. Young, in a letter to the *Times*, July 23, 1936, quoted in Jeremy Musson, "Eltham Palace, London," *Country Life* (June 17, 1999): 86.

51. For the City Temple at Holborn, see *The Builder*, December 19, 1958.

52. Ashbee a failure: Clive Aslet in conversation with the author, March 2012. Failure and tragedy: Clive Aslet, *The Last Country Houses* (New Haven: Yale University Press, 1982), 238–243; for the Beauchamp story, see the wonderful section in ibid., 250–255.

53. For Wells, see Mosette Broderick, *Triumvirate: McKim, Mead & White: Art, Architecture, Scandal and Class in America's Gilded Age* (New York: Alfred A. Knopf, 2010), 57–59, 276, 537.

54. See Richard Overy, *The Morbid Age: Britain and the Crisis of Civilization, 1919–1939* (London: Allen Lane, 2009), especially chapters 1 and 2.

55. Brian Appleyard, *Richard Rogers: A Biography* (London: Faber & Faber, 1986), 35.

56. Richard Giles, *Re-pitching the Tent* (Norwich: Canterbury Press, 2004, 3rd edn.), 134.

57. Ibid., unnumbered plates between 112 and 113.

58. Ibid., 109.

59. Roger W. Moss, *Historic Sacred Places of Philadelphia* (Philadelphia: University of Pennsylvania Press, 2005), 221. The beautiful interior of Wakefield cathedral in Yorkshire, a combination of relatively minor interventions by different designers over the last 150 years, is currently under threat of going the same way as Philadelphia: see Timothy Brittain-Catlin, "On Margate Sands / I Can Connect / Nothing with Nothing," *AA Files*, no. 63 (2011): 100–103.

60. The story is told in Deyan Sudjic, "Love It or Hate It, We Must Save the Commonwealth Institute," *Guardian*, June 18, 2006; online at: http://www.guardian.co.uk/artanddesign/2006/jun/18/architecture.communities.

61. At a meeting of the Victorian Society's Southern Buildings Sub-Committee which I attended as member, October 18, 2012.

62. Michael Yelton and John Salmon, *Anglican Church-Building in London 1915–1945* (Reading: Spire, 2007).

CHAPTER 4

1. The personal information on Pleydell-Bouverie comes from the section by Stone of an unpublished obituary, located in his biographical file at the RIBA Library.

2. Thomas F. Ford, biographical file in the RIBA Library.

3. Ramsgate Historical Society: http://www.facebook.com/note.php?note_id=207221895968221 and http://www.stmarkschurchramsgate.co.uk/history%201.htm.

4. Albert Williamson, "The Church of St Mark Northwood Ramsgate," photocopied typescript, 1993: available at Canterbury Cathedral Archives U3/283/28/1.

5. My thanks to Rev. Christopher Skingley for locating the drawings for me.

6. ICBS M1504 Folio 14ff.

7. Williamson, "St Mark," 100.

8. Ibid.

9. In April 1965: ibid., 83.

10. My thanks to Kurt Helfrich at the BAL, and especially to Edward Bottoms at the AA. My biographical information on Flaxman comes from my telephone interview with him, December 15, 2012.

11. http://www.publications.parliament.uk/pa/cm199293/cmhansrd/1992-11-26/Writtens-1.html.

12. Percival W. Flaxman, "Notes on three Danish Gardens," *Architectural Association Journal* (June 1951): 24. My thanks to Edward Bottoms for finding this.

13. See, for example, John Martin Robinson, *The Latest Country Houses* (London: Bodley Head, 1984), 136–142.

14. Obituary by M. J. Tree, *Architects' Journal* (September 5, 1973): 530.

15. Ulrik Plesner, *In Situ: An Architectural Memoir from Sri Lanka* (Copenhagen: Aristo, 2012), 25. Plesner gives the date as 1932, but it appears from other evidence to have been the year after.

16. Helen Ashton, *Bricks and Mortar* (London: Victor Gollancz, 1932), 291.

17. See http://www.pem.cam.ac.uk/the-college/pembroke-past-and-present/.

18. http://www.thebentallcentre-shopping.com/download_files/TBC_FACT%20GUIDE%20v4.pdf. No date, but post-1992.

19. http://www.imperial.ac.uk/college.asp?P=2970, 491; Bridget Cherry and Nikolaus Pevsner, *The Buildings of England: London 3: North West* (New Haven: Yale University Press, 2002), 491; Bridget Cherry and Nikolaus Pevsner, *The Buildings of England: London 2: South* (New Haven: Yale University Press, 2002), 313.

20. P. A. Barron, *The House Desirable: A Handbook for Those Who Wish to Acquire Homes that Charm* (London: Methuen, 1929), 7.

21. C. F. A. Voysey, *Individuality* (London: Chapman & Hall, 1915), 89. Pugin is said himself to have drawn 1,000 drawings for the chamber of the House of Lords alone.

22. Stanford Anderson's translation, from the revised edition of Muthesius's *Stilarchitektur und Baukunst*: Stanford Anderson, ed., *Style-Architecture and Building-Art: Transformations of Architecture in the Nineteenth Century and Its Present Condition / Hermann Muthesius* (Santa Monica: Getty Center for History of Art and the Humanities, 1994), 91–92.

23. Adolf Loos, "Vom armen reichen Mann," *Neues Wiener Tageblatt*, April 26, 1900.

24. David Watkin, *Radical Classicism: The Architecture of Quinlan Terry* (New York: Rizzoli, 2006), 15.

25. Basil Ionides, *Colour and Interior Decoration* (London: Country Life, 1926), 14.

26. See, for example, an article in the London *Daily Telegraph*, November 4, 2011: http://www.telegraph.co.uk/culture/tvandradio/downton-abbey/8868732/Downton-Abbey-historical-inaccuracies-and-mistakes-plaguing-ITV-show.html.

27. William Shakespeare, *King Lear*, Act II, Scene 4.

28. R. Randal Phillips, *The House Improved* (London: Country Life, 1931), viii.

29. Ibid., 22–23, 133, 15, 83.

30. Ibid., 46–51. The house is at 98 Hamilton Terrace: my thanks to Shirley and Romanos Brihi for tracking it down.

31. Ibid., 52–55, 110–115.

32. http://en.wikipedia.org/wiki/Howard_Spicer. References there cite the *New York Times*, August 18, 1926, and the Melbourne *Argos*, August 20, 1926.

33. For more on Bolton, see Jill Lever, "A. T. Bolton, Architect," *Architectural History* 27 (1984): 429–442.

34. Lawrence Weaver, *Small Country Houses of To-day* (London: Country Life, 1911), 17–22.

35. Hookerel: W. Shaw Sparrow, ed., *Flats, Urban Houses and Cottage Homes: A Companion Volume to "The British Home of To-day"* (London: Hodder & Stoughton, 1907), 138–140; Dawber's cottage is at Long Wittenham near Abingdon: it was published in both Britain (Anonymous, *The Smaller House: Being Selected Examples of the Latest Practice in Modern English Domestic Architecture* [London: Architecture Press, 1924], 68–71) and the USA (*American Architect*, 1923). The authors of the Berkshire "Pevsner" appear not to have known about the inside, as they describe the house as "not especially remarkable": Geoffrey Tyack, Simon Bradley, and Nikolaus Pevsner, *The Buildings of England: Berkshire* (New Haven: Yale University Press, 2010), 364.

36. The interiors of the infirmary were designed by Steffian Bradley Architects, specialists in medical interiors.

37. Watkin addressed the doleful impact that popular archaeology has had on the history of architecture in his book on the Roman Forum, giving the example of the way in which archaeologists like to leave uncovered ancient foundations exposed in spite of their ugliness: see, for example, his *The Roman Forum* (London: Profile: 2009), 118–119, 123.

CHAPTER 5

1. P. A. Barron, *The House Desirable: A Handbook for Those Who Wish to Acquire Homes that Charm* (London: Methuen, 1929), 3.

2. Clough Williams-Ellis, *England and the Octopus* (London: Godfrey Bles, 1928), 15.

3. Todd W. Bressi, "Planning the American Dream," in Peter Katz, *The New Urbanism: Toward an Architecture of Community* (New York: McGraw-Hill, 1994), xxxv.

4. Peter Katz, *The New Urbanism: Toward an Architecture of Community* (New York: McGraw-Hill, 1994), x.

5. Bressi, "Planning the American Dream," xxxvi.

6. See Frances Mikuriya's unpublished doctoral dissertation, "Duchy Unoriginal: The Prince of Wales and Architecture," Architectural Association School of Architecture, London, 2011. Mikuriya adds that in her opinion the Prince regarded modernism between the 1960s and 1980s as if it were a kind of spreading disease.

7. Horst and Tim Street-Porter, "A Tale of One Coach-House and Two Ingenious Architects," *House & Garden* (London) (June 1979): 96, 98. My thanks to Mosette Broderick for locating the house, and to Robert Stern and Peter Morris Dixon, of Robert A. M. Stern Architects, for their assistance and comments.

8. Roger Scruton, *Beauty: A Very Short Introduction* (Oxford: Oxford University Press, 2011), 69.

9. Muriel Spark, "The Go-Away Bird," in *The Go-Away Bird and Other Stories* (London: Macmillan, 1958), 96–97.

BIBLIOGRAPHY

Allibone, Jill. *George Devey Architect, 1820–1886*. Cambridge, UK: Lutterworth Press, 1991.

Anderson, Stanford, ed. *Style Architecture and Building Art: Transformations of Architecture in the Nineteenth Century and its Present Condition / Hermann Muthesius*. Santa Monica: Getty Center for History of Art and the Humanities, 1994.

Anonymous. *The Smaller House: Being Selected Examples of the Latest Practice in Modern English Domestic Architecture*. London: Architecture Press, 1924.

Appleyard, Brian. *Richard Rogers: A Biography*. London: Faber & Faber, 1986.

Arnold, Damian. "Jan Wanted to Do Extraordinary Things." *Architects' Journal* (January 22, 2009): 10–12.

Ashton, Helen. *Bricks and Mortar*. London: Victor Gollancz, 1932.

Aslet, Clive. *The Last Country Houses*. New Haven: Yale University Press, 1982.

Aslet, Clive. "An Interview with the Late Paul Paget 1901–1985." *Thirties Society Journal*, no. 6 (1987): 16–25.

Ballantyne, Andrew, and Andrew Law. "Tudoresque." In *Pursuit of the Ideal Home*. London: Reaktion, 2011.

Banham, Reyner. "The New Brutalism." *Architectural Review* (December 1955): 855–861.

Banham, Reyner. "The Style: 'Flimsy . . . Effeminate?" In *A Tonic to the Nation: The Festival of Britain 1951*, ed. Mary Banham and Bevis Hillier, 190–198. London: Thames & Hudson, 1976.

Barron, P. A. *The House Desirable: A Handbook for Those Who Wish to Acquire Homes that Charm*. London: Methuen, 1929.

Bartholomew, Alfred. *Specifications for Practical Architecture, Preceded by an Essay on the Decline of Excellence in the Structure and in the Science of Modern English Buildings, with the Proposal of Remedies for those Defects*. London: John Williams, 1840.

Belcher, Margaret. *The Collected Letters of A. W. N. Pugin*. Vol. 2. Oxford: Oxford University Press, 2003.

Benson, E. F. *Mapp and Lucia*. 1935; London: Penguin, 2004.

Blaker, Catriona. *Edward Pugin and Kent*. Ramsgate: Pugin Society, 2003.

Blundell Jones, Peter. "Richmond Riverside: Sugaring the Pill." *Architectural Review* (November 1988): 86–90.

Blundell Jones, Peter. "Between Tradition and Modernity: The Reticent Architecture of David Lea." *Spazio e Società*, no. 55 (October/December 1991): 12–27.

Blundell Jones, Peter. "Traditional Values." *Architectural Review* (August 1993): 45–50.

Blundell Jones, Peter. *Peter Hübner: Building as a Social Process / Peter Hübner: Bauen als sozialer Prozeß*. Fellbach: Axel Menges, 2007.

Borg, Malcolm. *British Colonial Architecture, Malta 1800–1900*. San Gwann, Malta: Publishers Enterprise Group, 2001.

Bowen, Elizabeth. *Eva Trout*. 1969; London: Vintage, 1999.

Bressi, Vincent. "Planning the American Dream." In Peter Katz, *The New Urbanism: Toward an Architecture of Community*, xxv–xlii. New York: McGraw-Hill, 1994.

Brett, Lionel. "Detail on the South Bank." *Design*, no. 32 (1951): 2–7.

Brittain-Catlin, Timothy. "Gunnar Asplund, by Peter Blundell Jones." *AA Files*, no. 53 (2006): 77–82.

Brittain-Catlin, Timothy. *The English Parsonage in the Early Nineteenth Century*. Reading: Spire, 2008.

Brittain-Catlin, Timothy. "Cabin Class." *The World of Interiors* (April 2009): 162–165.

Brittain-Catlin, Timothy. "Horace Field and Lloyds Bank." *Architectural History* 53 (2010): 271–294.

Brittain-Catlin, Timothy. *Leonard Manasseh and Partners*. London: RIBA Publishing, 2010.

Brittain-Catlin, Timothy. "Downward Trajectory: Towards a Theory of Failure." *Architecture Research Quarterly* 15 (3) (2011): 139–147.

Brittain-Catlin, Timothy. "On Margate Sands / I Can Connect / Nothing with Nothing." *AA Files*, no. 63 (2011): 100–103.

Broderick, Mosette. *Triumvirate: McKim, Mead & White: Art, Architecture, Scandal and Class in America's Gilded Age*. New York: Alfred A. Knopf, 2010.

Brooks, Chris. *The Gothic Revival*. London: Phaidon, 1999.

Burfield, Diana. *Edward Cresy 1792–1858: Architect and Civil Engineer*. Donington: Shaun Tyas, 2003.

Calder, Barnabas. "'A Terrible Battle with Architecture': Denys Lasdun in the 1950s, Part 2." *Architectural Research Quarterly* 12 (1) (2008): 59–68.

Cherry, Bridget, and Nikolaus Pevsner. *The Buildings of England: London 3: North West*. New Haven: Yale University Press, 2002.

Cherry, Bridget, and Nikolaus Pevsner. *The Buildings of England: London 2: South.* New Haven: Yale University Press, 2002.

Colvin, Howard. *A Biographical Dictionary of British Architects 1600–1840.* 3rd edn. New Haven: Yale University Press, 1995.

Crampton, Paul. *Canterbury's Lost Heritage.* Stroud: Sutton, 2006.

Cunningham, Michael. *By Nightfall.* London: Fourth Estate, 2010.

Dakers, Caroline. *The Holland Park Circle: Artists in Victorian Society.* New Haven: Yale University Press, 1999.

Dal Co, Francesco, Kurt W. Forster, and Hadley Arnold. *Frank O. Gehry: The Complete Works.* New York: Monacelli Press, 1998.

Darling, Elizabeth. *Wells Coates.* London: RIBA Publishing, 2012.

Davey, Peter. "Outrage: Blue Blob in Birmingham." *Architectural Review* (October 2003): 24–25.

Dean, David. *The Thirties: Recalling the English Architectural Scene.* London: Trefoil, 1983.

Ditchfield, P. H. *The Charm of the English Village.* London: Batsford, 1908.

Ditchfield, P. H. *The Manor Houses of England.* London: Batsford, 1910.

Dolkart, Andrew. *The Row House Reborn: Architecture and Neighborhoods in New York City, 1908–1929.* Baltimore: Johns Hopkins University Press, 2009.

Dorrel, Ed. "'Future Systems' Selfridges under Attack over Lack of Natural Lighting." *Architects' Journal* (July 10, 2003): 12.

Fawcett, Bill. *The North Eastern Railway's Two Palaces of Business.* York: Friends of the National Railway Museum, 2001.

Field, Horace, and Michael Bunney. *English Domestic Architecture of the XVII and XVIII Centuries: A Selection of Examples of Smaller Buildings / Measured, Drawn and Photographed, with an Introduction and Notes by Horace Field and Michael Bunney.* London: George Bell, 1905; 2nd edn. 1928.

Field, Horace. "Architectural Reminiscences—no. 14." *Builder* (October 11, 1946): 370.

Flaxman, Percival W. "Notes on Three Danish Gardens." *Architectural Association Journal* (June 1951): 24–30.

Foges, Chris. "Making Sense of Place." *Architecture Today* (October 2012): 8–11.

Frampton, Kenneth. *Modern Architecture: A Critical History.* 2nd edn. London: Thames & Hudson, 1985.

Garner, Thomas. *The Domestic Architecture of England During the Tudor Period.* Introduction by Arthur Stratton. London: Batsford, 1911.

Gerrish, Helena. *Edwardian Country Life: The Story of H. Avray Tipping.* London: Frances Lincoln, 2011.

Giles, Richard. *Re-pitching the Tent.* 3rd edn. Norwich: Canterbury Press, 2004.

Girouard, Mark. *Sweetness and Light: The "Queen Anne" Movement 1860–1900*. Oxford: Oxford University Press, 1977.

Girouard, Mark. *Elizabethan Architecture: Its Rise and Fall, 1540–1640*. New Haven: Yale University Press for the Paul Mellon Centre for British Art, 2009.

Glendinning, Miles. *Architecture's Evil Empire: The Triumph and Tragedy of Global Modernism*. London: Reaktion, 2010.

Goodhart-Rendel, H. S. *English Architecture since the Regency: An Interpretation*. London: Constable, 1953.

Gray, A. Stuart. *Edwardian Architecture: A Biographical Dictionary*. London: Duckworth, 1985.

Gwilt, Joseph. *An Encyclopaedia of Architecture, Historical, Theoretical and Practical*. London: Longman, Brown, Green, and Longman, 1842.

Habershon, Matthew. *The Ancient Half-Timbered Houses of England*. London: John Weale, 1836–1839.

Harris, Alexandra. *Romantic Moderns: English Writers, Artists and the Imagination from Virginia Woolf to John Piper*. London: Thames & Hudson, 2010.

Hart-Davis, Rupert. *Hugh Walpole: A Biography*. London: Macmillan, 1952.

Harwood, Elain, and Alan Powers. *Tayler and Green Architects 1938–1973: The Spirit of Place in Modern Housing*. London: The Prince of Wales's Institute of Architecture, 1998.

Harwood, Elain, and Alan Powers. "From Downtown to Diversity: Revisiting the 1970s." In *Twentieth Century Architecture 10: The Seventies*, ed. Elain Harwood and Alan Powers, 9–35. London: Twentieth Century Society, 2012.

Heinze-Greenberg, Ita. "We'll Leave It to the Schultzes from Naumburg to Ignore the Mediterranean as the Father of the International Art of Composition." In *Erich Mendelsohn, Dynamics and Function: Realized Visions of a Cosmopolitan Architect*, ed. Regina Stephan, 182–189. Ostfildern-Ruit: IFA, 1999.

Hess, Alan, and Alan Weintraub. *The Architecture of John Lautner*. London: Thames & Hudson, 1999.

Higgott, Andrew. *Mediating Modernism: Architectural Cultures in Britain*. Abingdon: Routledge, 2007.

Hill, Rosemary. *God's Architect: Pugin and the Building of Romantic Britain*. London: Penguin, 2007.

Hollinghurst, Alan. *The Stranger's Child*. London: Picador, 2011.

Horst, and Tim Street-Porter [photographers: no author name]. "A Tale of One Coach-House and Two Ingenious Architects." *House & Garden* (London) (June 1979): 96–101.

Howell, W. G. "Edward Reynolds" (obituary). *Architectural Association Journal* (February 1959): 218.

Hussey, Christopher. "Eltham Hall." *Country Life* (May 15, 1937): 534–539; (May 22, 1937): 568–573; (May 29, 1937): 594–599.

Hyland, Gerard. "The E. W. Pugin Gazetteer Part 2." *True Principles, the Journal of The Pugin Society* 3, no. 5 (Autumn 2008): 45–55.

Hyland, Gerard. "Edward Welby Pugin, Architect, 1834–75." *True Principles, the Journal of The Pugin Society* 4, no. 1 (Autumn 2009): 51–55.

Ionides, Basil. *Colour and Interior Decoration*. London: Country Life, 1926.

James, Kathleen. *Erich Mendelsohn and the Architecture of German Modernism*. Cambridge: Cambridge University Press, 1997.

Jencks, Charles. *Modern Movements in Architecture*. Harmondsworth: Penguin, 1973.

Katz, Peter. *The New Urbanism: Toward an Architecture of Community*. New York: McGraw-Hill, 1994.

Kehoe, Louise. *In This Dark House*. Harmondsworth: Penguin, 1997.

Lancaster, Osbert. *A Cartoon History of Architecture*. 1938–1959; London: John Murray, 1975.

Lamster, Mark. "181 Renoirs, 69 Cézannes, 59 Matisses and 46 Picassos." *Architectural Review*, August 2012: 59–65.

Lever, Jill. "A.T. Bolton, Architect." *Architectural History* 27 (1984): 429–442.

Long, Kieran. "Do Malls Really Excite Us Any More?" *Icon* (September 2003): 126–132.

Loos, Adolf, "Vom armen reichen Mann [The Poor Little Rich Man]". *Neues Wiener Tageblatt*, April 26, 1900.

Loudon, J. C. *An Encyclopaedia of Cottage, Farm, and Villa Architecture and Furniture*. London: Longman, 1833.

Lurie, Alison. *Not in Front of the Grown-Ups*. London: Sphere Books, 1991.

Mandler, Peter. *The Fall and Rise of the Stately Home*. New Haven: Yale University Press, 1997.

Menuge, Adam. *Oxburgh Hall, Oxborough, Norfolk: A Survey and Investigation of the Moated House*. London: English Heritage, 2006.

Metzger-Szmuk, Nitza. *Batim min hachol: adrikhalut hasignon habeinleumi beTel Aviv, 1931–1948*. Tel Aviv: Ministry of Defence, 1994.

Mikuriya, Frances. "Duchy Unoriginal: The Prince of Wales and Architecture." Doctoral dissertation, 2011. Architectural Association School of Architecture, London.

Moss, Roger W. *Historic Sacred Places of Philadelphia*. Philadelphia: University of Pennsylvania Press, 2005.

Musson, Jeremy. "Eltham Palace, London." *Country Life* (London, England) 17 (June 1999): 86–91.

Nash, Joseph. *The Mansions of England in the Olden Time*. London: T. McLean, 1839–1849.

Newman, John. *The Buildings of England: North East and East Kent*. 3rd edn. Harmondsworth: Penguin, 1983.

Oliver, Paul, Ian Davis, and Ian Bentley. *Dunroamin: The Suburban Semi and Its Enemies.* London: Barrie & Jenkins, 1981.

Overy, Richard. *The Morbid Age: Britain and the Crisis of Civilization, 1919–1939.* London: Allen Lane, 2009.

Pevsner, Nikolaus. *The Buildings of England: London: Volume One, The Cities of London and Westminster.* 3rd edn. Harmondsworth: Penguin, 1973.

Pevsner, Nikolaus. "Goodhart-Rendel's Roll-Call." In *Edwardian Architecture and Its Origins*, ed. Alastair Service, 472–483. London: Architectural Press, 1975.

Pevsner, Nikolaus. *Pioneers of Modern Design: From William Morris to Walter Gropius.* Harmondsworth: Penguin, 1960.

Pevsner, Nikolaus, and David Neave. *The Buildings of England: Yorkshire: York and the East Riding.* 2nd edn. New Haven: Yale University Press, 2005.

Pevsner, Nikolaus, Elizabeth Williamson, and Geoffrey K. Brandwood. *The Buildings of England: Buckinghamshire.* London: Penguin, 1994.

Pevsner, Nikolaus, and Bill Wilson. *Norfolk 2: North West and South.* London: Penguin, 1999.

Phillips, Alan, "Spoken into the Bloid." *Architecture Today* (October 2003): 56–71.

Phillips, Randal. *The House Improved.* London: Country Life, 1931.

Plesner, Ulrik. *In Situ: An Architectural Memoir from Sri Lanka.* Copenhagen: Aristo, 2012.

Powell, Christabel. *Augustus Pugin, Designer of the British Houses of Parliament.* Lampeter: Edwin Mellen Press, 2006.

Powell, Kenneth. *Edward Cullinan Architects.* London: Academy Editions, 1995.

Powell, Kenneth. "Erith in Context." In *Raymond Erith: Progressive Classicist 1904–1973*, ed. Lucy Archer, 19–26. London: Sir John Soane's Museum, 2004.

Powers, Alan. *Britain.* London: Reaktion, 2007.

Prak, Niels L. *Architects: The Noted and the Ignored.* Chichester: John Wiley & Sons, 1984.

Pugin, A. W. N. *Contrasts, or a Parallel between the Noble Edifices of the Middle Ages, and the Corresponding buildings of the Present day; shewing the Present Decay of Taste.* 2nd edn. London: Charles Dolman, 1841.

Pugin, A. W. N. *The True Principles of Pointed or Christian Architecture.* London: John Weale, 1841.

Pugin, A. W. N. *An Apology for the Revival of Christian Architecture.* London: John Weale, 1843.

Richards, J. M. "The Hollow Victory: 1932–1972." *RIBA Journal* (May 1972): 192–197.

Richards, J. M. *Memoirs of an Unjust Fella.* London: Weidenfeld & Nicolson, 1980.

Ridley, Jane. *The Architect and His Wife: A Life of Edwin Lutyens.* London: Chatto & Windus, 2002.

Robinson, John Martin. *The Latest Country Houses*. London: Bodley Head, 1984.

Robinson, John Martin. *James Wyatt, 1746–1813: Architect to George III*. London: Paul Mellon Centre for Studies in British Art, 2012.

Rolef, Susan Hattis. "The Knesset Building in Giv'at Ram—Planning and Construction." Originally published in Hebrew in *Cathedra* (*Journal for Holy Land Studies*) 96, Yad Izhak Ben-Zvi, Jerusalem, July 2002; English language version available at http://www.knesset.gov.il/building/architecture/eng/article1_eng.htm

Ross, Alex. *The Rest Is Noise: Listening to the Twentieth Century*. London: Harper Perennial, 2009.

Rouart, Jean-Marie. *La noblesse des vaincus*. Paris: Grasset, 1997.

Saint, Andrew. *Architect and Engineer: A Study in Sibling Rivalry*. New Haven: Yale University Press, 2007.

Saint, Andrew. *Richard Norman Shaw*. New Haven: Yale University Press, 2010.

Saumarez Smith, Charles. *The Building of Castle Howard*. London: Faber & Faber, 1990.

Scruton, Roger. *Beauty: A Very Short Introduction*. Oxford: Oxford University Press, 2011.

Scully, Vincent. "The Architecture of Community." In Peter Katz, *The New Urbanism: Toward an Architecture of Community*, 221–230. New York: McGraw-Hill, 1994.

Smithson, Alison. "House in Soho." *Architectural Design* (December 1953): 342.

Spark, Muriel. "The Go-Away Bird." In *The Go-Away Bird and Other Stories*, 74–137. London: Macmillan, 1958.

Sparrow, W. Shaw, ed. *Flats, Urban Houses and Cottage Homes: A Companion Volume to "The British Home of To-day."* London: Hodder & Stoughton, 1907.

Spencer, Christopher, and Geoffrey Wilson. *Elbow Room: The Story of John Sydney Brocklesby, Arts and Crafts Architect*. London: Ainsworth and Nelson in conjunction with Christopher Spencer, Graystones Press and Dasprint Ltd., 1984.

Stadler, Laurent. "'New Brutalism', 'Topology' and 'Image': Some Remarks on the Architectural Debates in England around 1950." *Journal of Architecture* 13 (3) (June 2008): 263–281.

Stamp, Gavin. *The Great Perspectivists*. London: Trefoil Books, 1982.

Stamp, Gavin. *An Architect of Promise: George Gilbert Scott Junior (1839–1897) and the Late Gothic Revival*. Donington: Shaun Tyas, 2002.

Stamp, Gavin. "Neo-Tudor and Its Enemies." *Architectural History* 49 (2006): 1–33.

Stephan, Regina. "One of the Most Lovable People and at the Same Time One of the Most Unpleasant: Mendelsohn and His Assistants in the 1920s and Early 1930s." In *Erich Mendelsohn, Dynamics and Function: Realized Visions of a Cosmopolitan Architect*, ed. Regina Stephan, 152–158. Ostfildern-Ruit: IFA, 1999.

Sudjic, Deyan. "Love It or Hate It, We Must Save the Commonwealth Institute." *Guardian*, June 18, 2006; online at http://www.guardian.co.uk/artanddesign/2006/jun/18/architecture.communities.

Sudjic, Deyan. *Norman Foster: A Life in Architecture*. London: Weidenfeld & Nicolson, 2010.

Summerfield, Adam. "Rethinking Medway—a Proposal for Democratic Participation in the Development of Chatham Waterfront." Undergraduate dissertation, University of Kent, Canterbury, 2008.

Till, Jeremy. "The Architecture of the Impure Community." In *Occupying Architecture: Between the Architect and the User*, ed. Jonathan Hill, 61–75. London: Routledge, 1998.

Till, Jeremy. *Architecture Depends*. Cambridge, Mass: MIT Press, 2009.

Tyack, Geoffrey, Simon Bradley, and Nikolaus Pevsner. *The Buildings of England: Berkshire*. New Haven: Yale University Press, 2010.

Voysey, C. F. A. "Ideas in Things." In *The Arts Connected with Building*, ed. T. Raffles Davison, 101–137. London: Batsford, 1909.

Voysey, C. F. A. *Individuality*. London: Chapman & Hall, 1915.

Wahrhaftig, Myra. *They Laid the Foundation: Lives and Works of German-Speaking Jewish Architects in Palestine 1918–1948*. Berlin: Wasmuth, 2007.

Walpole, Hugh. *Rogue Herries*. 1930; London: Frances Lincoln, 2008.

Watkin, David. *Morality and Architecture*. Oxford: Oxford University Press, 1977.

Watkin, David. *Radical Classicism: The Architecture of Quinlan Terry*. New York: Rizzoli, 2006.

Watkin, David. *Visions of World Architecture*. Exh. cat. London: Sir John Soane's Museum, 2007.

Watkin, David. *The Roman Forum*. London: Profile, 2009.

Weaver, Lawrence. *Small Country Houses of To-day*. London: Country Life, 1911.

Webster, Christopher. *R. D. Chantrell (1793–1872) and the Architecture of a Lost Generation*. Reading: Spire, 2010.

Williams, Owen. "Architecture—Trade, Profession or Calling." *Architectural Association Journal* (January 1953): 98–105.

Williams-Ellis, Clough. *England and the Octopus*. London: Godfrey Bles, 1928.

Williamson, Albert. "The Church of St Mark Northwood Ramsgate." Photocopied typescript, 1993, available at Canterbury Cathedral Archives U3/283/28/1.

Wittkower, Rudolf and Margot. *Born under Saturn*. London: Weidenfeld & Nicolson, 1963.

Woodman, Ellis. "Bull Market." *Building Design* (September 5, 2003): 13–17.

Wright, Frank Lloyd. *An Autobiography*. 3rd edn. London: Quartet, 1977.

Yelton, Michael, and John Salmon. *Anglican Church-building in London 1915–1945*. Reading: Spire, 2007.

INDEX